JUNGLE FIGHTERS

JUNGLE FIGHTERS

A GI Correspondent's Experiences in the New Guinea Campaign

Jules Archer

JULIAN MESSNER   NEW YORK

34626

All rights reserved
including the right of reproduction
in whole or in part in any form.
Published by Julian Messner,
A Division of Simon & Schuster, Inc.
Simon & Schuster Building
Rockefeller Center
1230 Avenue of the Americas
New York, New York 10020

JULIAN MESSNER and colophon are
trademarks of Simon & Schuster, Inc.

10 9 8 7 6 5 4 3 2 1

Manufactured in the United States of America

Design by Teresa Delgado, A Good Thing Inc.

Library of Congress Cataloging in Publication Data

Archer, Jules.
  Jungle fighters.

  Includes index.
  Summary: An account of the military campaign in New
Guinea during World War II, which the author viewed from
several positions, including staff sergeant and war
correspondent.
  1. World War, 1939–1945—Campaigns—New Guinea—
Juvenile literature. 2. Archer, Jules—Juvenile litera-
ture. 3. World War, 1939–1945—Personal narratives,
American—Juvenile literature. 4. World War, 1939–1945—
Jungle warfare—Juvenile literature. 5. New Guinea—
History—Juvenile literature. [1. World War, 1939–1945—
Campaigns—New Guinea. 2. Archer, Jules. 3. World War,
1939–1945—Personal narratives, American. 4. World War,
1939–1945—Jungle warfare] I. Title.
D767.95.A64   1985   940.54'26   84-29465
ISBN 0-671-46058-7 (lib. bdg.)

For
my newest grandchildren
Colleen Archer
Cameron Maxwell Archer
and
Erin Archer
May they never have to live through
experiences like those described in this book

CONTENTS

Introduction

The last war in which we were involved that most Americans agreed was fully justified was World War II, the war against the aggressive Axis powers, Nazi Germany, Fascist Italy, and imperial Japan. Unlike the later controversial war in Vietnam, World War II commanded almost total popular support, particularly after the Japanese attack on Pearl Harbor.

This book deals with our military campaign in that war in far-off New Guinea, which at the time was a League of Nations mandate administered by our ally, Australia. After the Japanese attacked Pearl Harbor, Hawaii, on December 7, 1941, their armies quickly swept over the South Pacific, seeking to conquer all of Asia, including Australia, before we could raise forces to stop them.

Our most famous general, Douglas MacArthur, was driven out of the Philippines when the Japanese overran the islands. President Franklin D. Roosevelt ordered him to escape to Australia to take command of the Allied land and air forces in the South Pacific. But he was given only token American and British units with which to oppose the powerful military machine of the Japanese in the Pacific war theater. Because the European theater of war had priority, most American troops, planes, tanks, and ships were being rushed to England to stop Japan's allies, Hitler and Mussolini.

In the early stages of the Pacific war, all MacArthur was expected to do with his slim forces was fight a holding action to prevent the Japanese from conquering

8

Australia. The key to that continent's defense was the island of New Guinea, which sits just above the northeast tip of Australia. If the Japanese won control of New Guinea, they could use the island as an air, naval, and staging base. They would then be able to cut off all supplies and reinforcements from the United States and launch a powerful invasion of Australia.

To save Australia it was imperative that the Japanese be stopped on the dragon-shaped island of New Guinea and then driven out. For that purpose MacArthur rushed a small task force to Milne Bay, where the Coral Sea rounded the southeast tip of the island.

Milne Bay, jungle site of the largest coconut plantations in the world, had only a small dirt airstrip, a few dirt roads, and two or three primitive jetties. Here MacArthur planned to establish an airfield base for bomber and fighter planes that could attack enemy invasion convoys as they rounded the tip of New Guinea to attack Australia.

I was a member of the task force sent to Milne Bay. I was a master sergeant in an aircraft warning company attached to the Fifth Air Force. I was also authorized as a war correspondent by order of General MacArthur. Our task force was told candidly that we were "expendable"—meaning that we were not expected to survive our mission, but were considered a necessary sacrifice in order to delay the Japanese advance southward.

We had good reason not to expect to return alive from New Guinea. Up to this point in the war, the Japanese had been victorious in every campaign they had fought in the Pacific. The never-defeated Japanese marines who had spearheaded all these victories were now leading the invasion forces landing all along the eastern coast of New Guinea.

Our inexperienced troops were plunged into a strange and different war, fighting in a jungle among a primitive Melanesian people, some tribes of which were head-hunters. This book tells the story of how we endured in the distant jungle that was our home for nearly four years.

I was inducted into the Army while we were still at peace in October 1941. But after Pearl Harbor, our basic training in South Carolina was cut short and my company was rushed north to become an urgently needed aircraft warning unit, destined for the Pacific. I was offered a choice of either going overseas or staying behind to go to officers' candidate school. I chose to go overseas. I was made a staff sergeant and shortly afterward a master sergeant.

Whatever our skills or talents in civilian life, we could be sure of doing something totally different in the Army. An old-line Army sergeant explained to me, "There are only two ways to do things—your way, which is the wrong way, and the Army way." The Army preferred to train recruits from scratch. That was how skiers like me ended up in tropical jungles.

For some youths, fighting in a war overseas held the appeal of a dashing adventure. But they found the personal cost heavier than they realized, even apart from the risk to life and limb. The loneliness of separation from their loved ones weighed heavily on their spirits. And the ordeal of combat inspired numbing fear. We never got used to shells and bombs screaming down on us from the sky, or to planes strafing us at treetop level.

Fighting a war—even a just war like ours—was often disillusioning as well as frightening. We became aware of tragic blunders of command that snuffed out the lives of our comrades. It was devastating when some of those casualties were personal friends. Many of us came to feel that, to top generals in Washington or the rear echelon, we soldiers were just so many colored pins on a map, to be moved around as war strategy required.

But to us a regiment was not simply a military unit. It was three thousand men, one at a time—each man with his own private world, loved ones at home, and hopes for the future.

During my years overseas, I had the opportunity to observe officer–enlisted man relationships from inside two different branches of the service: the Signal Corps, my first affiliation, and the Air Corps to which I transferred. I found that officers' abuses of power were frequent in my first outfit, but almost nonexistent in my Air Corps unit, which enjoyed a far greater spirit of democracy and a much higher morale.

I felt strongly about the importance of morale because even a just war can be an abomination if soldiers resent those who lead them. No war is glorious. It is ugly; often dreary, uncomfortable, and miserable. And no matter how just the cause, war brutalizes those who fight in it.

Combat makes men desperate. When your own life is at stake, it is difficult not to subscribe to the law of the jungle—kill or be killed. In our case the battlefield *was* the jungle. The invisible enemy, hidden behind tall kunai grass and entangled vines, bombing our camps every night, sought to kill as many of us as possible. At war it was hard to think of the Japanese as basically decent people like ourselves.

For GIs in World War II, learning to adjust to life in the jungle was difficult. Each day was often sheer misery, especially during the rainy season, when they were trying to survive in dripping tents on field rations. As bad as it was for us, the agony of footsloggers in the infantry was far worse.

War is not parades, cheering, and flag waving.

There is much speculation today that there will be no more wars like World War II because of nuclear weapons, which can end a conflict—and possibly civilization—in an hour.

11

One can only hope that common sense will prevail, and that all nuclear weapons will be outlawed by the world community, just as all nations have agreed not to use chemical warfare. With much of the world in turmoil, it is too much to hope that war itself will be outlawed any time soon, even though the vast majority of the world's people cry out for peace.

This book is written to tell young Americans at or approaching draft age honestly what war is like, in the hope that they will never have to find out for themselves.

Jules Archer
Santa Cruz, California

1
Convoy

At the age of twenty-six, on October 2, 1941, I was ordered to report for Army service to Fort Dix, New Jersey. On the train to the induction center, a red-haired youth complained to me bitterly about the sacrifice required of young men like ourselves, while civilian workers and big business prospered from the defense buildup. Some recruits, gloomily convinced that they were doomed to be killed in uniform, passed around bottles of liquor and arrived at camp drunk.

No one was very gung-ho about military service before Pearl Harbor.

Our first meal in camp was stew, carrots, sweet pickle,

bread, and lemonade. The following morning we lined up for reveille and breakfast in pouring rain, which dripped down our collars as it had dripped through our barrack ceiling all night.

After two weeks at Fort Dix I was transferred to Camp Croft, South Carolina, for basic training. My first shock at the severity of Army life came when a fellow GI who had treated himself to a "baldy" haircut was punished by three grueling weeks of dawn-to-dusk K.P. (kitchen police) and, after staggering off duty, was forced to run around the battalion with a full field pack.

I was ordered to shave my mustache because the battalion commander did not wear one. Any GI who set down his rifle incorrectly or dropped it was punished by weekend K.P.

We were marched with full field packs under a blazing sun until some soldiers collapsed. We were then made to perform calisthenics with our heavy rifles until our arms could not lift them.

We quickly learned GI proverbs that were meant to save recruits from unnecessary misery. "Never volunteer" was one of these adages. A man who answered a call for "those with engineering or water projects experience" found himself, Johnny-mop in hand, cleaning out the latrines. To avoid being singled out for such unpleasant tasks, GI wisdom advocated positioning oneself, when possible, in a formation's back row.

I discovered early on that honesty was not a highly esteemed virtue in the Army. One day my heel accidentally caught on a stack of three rifles, tipping them over. The colonel in charge of the regiment asked my platoon who was responsible. No brother GI "squealed," but I owned up, believing that my honesty would at least mitigate my offense.

Instead, I was confined to camp for a weekend of K.P., fourteen hours of backbreaking, exhausting toil, with only one fifteen-minute rest.

14

We were put through bayonet drills with partners, taking turns lunging at each other in simulated bayonet attacks, to work up a blood lust. We spent a day charging through tear-gas chambers wearing gas masks, to teach us how to function in battle in case of enemy gas attacks.

Little sympathy was shown any GI who could not measure up to the grueling training program. One poor wretch could barely run; how he had even been drafted baffled us. His slow gait when ordered to double-time infuriated a lieutenant, who was convinced he was faking. He was ordered to run around the battalion area five times, nonstop, carrying a heavy sack of grenades. He collapsed and had to be hospitalized.

When one soldier mislaid his M-1 rifle, his whole platoon was awakened at midnight and ordered to search for it. Beds were stripped, mattresses turned, and footlockers emptied. The platoon was spared marching in a downpour to the firing range to search for it in the dark when the GI in question remembered where he had mislaid it.

Awakened in the freezing South Carolina dawn, some GIs couldn't cope with the frantic rush to dress in full field uniform, fall out for roll call at reveille, and then make their beds perfectly in time for inspection. One despairing soldier in my squad slept fully clothed *under* his bed, so that he could make the formation in time with his bed unrumpled.

The Army rationale for the hardships we underwent in basic training was that they were necessary to toughen us for the rigors of military service. Civilians were considered "soft" and "undisciplined." The harshness, injustices, and ordeals we were exposed to were supposed to break our spirit and make us instantly and unthinkingly obedient to orders, out of fear of severe punishment. To a large extent this purpose was accomplished, but only at the cost of making us hate Army life.

Things moved with lightning speed after the Japanese attack on Pearl Harbor on December 7, 1941. We shed no tears when our three-month training program was cut short by a month, even though leaving Camp Croft could have been construed as jumping out of the frying pan into the fire.

Combat, we all felt, couldn't be worse than Croft.

I had volunteered for the ski troops before Pearl Harbor and had been notified that I'd been accepted. But that arrangement was cancelled when top priority was given to the formation of aircraft warning units, which were urgently needed for our forces overseas. We were rushed back to Fort Dix as a Signal Corps company, designated as a combat-zone Fighter Sector unit attached to the Air Corps.

My company arrived in Fort Dix on a fiercely cold, snowy morning. In tents smelling of mildew, we huddled on cots in our overcoats, our breath vaporized, waiting for orders. A corporal poked his head in the tent and asked why we hadn't lit a fire in the stove.

"Nobody told us to," replied a surprised soldier. Our training had crushed our normal spirit of self-reliance to such an extent that none of us dared do anything without an order.

The captain of our company selected the three men with the highest I.Q. scores and appointed them acting noncoms. That was how I became a staff sergeant after only two months in the Army.

Our company was placed on alert and awaited orders to proceed to a port of embarkation. On appointing me acting first sergeant, the company adjutant ordered me to round up all the men and get them to the camp hospital immediately for foreign-service shots. I ran along rows of snowbound tents and mustered all GIs who were not on pass. Then I phoned the motor pool for transportation, and the men were hauled off to the hospital.

A major rushed up to me and demanded, "Sergeant, are you the one who ordered the men from this outfit to the hospital?" When I said I was, he screamed, "Who in blazes gave you that stupid order? Don't you know that this whole company is confined to camp? Get those men back from the hospital immediately! *Immediately*, do you hear?"

I sped to the phone in the orderly tent and told the hospital to return the men of my company as soon as they showed up. When the trucks came back with the men, the company adjutant summoned me, his face furious.

"Sergeant," he hissed, "who told you to order our men back from the hospital? Do you realize that doctors are waiting there right now to give them their shots?"

"A major gave me the order, sir."

"I don't care *who* told you to do it. You're *my* sergeant, and you will obey *my* orders! Now phone the hospital that you're sending the men back immediately!"

Like a scene in a television comedy, the major and the adjutant kept dashing in, countermanding the other's orders, then dashing out again. Two trucks rushed the men back and forth between the hospital and camp area

Fort Dix: the three privates with the highest IQs are chosen as Staff Sergeants. Author is in the center.

four times. Finally the company clerk called me to the phone. A doctor's voice at the other end was so loud that I had to hold the receiver away.

"Sergeant, are you *crazy*? Your men have dressed and undressed here four times without getting shots! I warn you and whatever crazy officer is giving these orders that if you pull those men back just once more, next time they show up we're going to throw them out bodily. *Do you hear me*?"

By 11:00 P.M., mercifully, the unidentified major gave up, and the men finally received their shots. Then their truck drivers, by now a relief crew, got lost and wandered around the vastness of Fort Dix trying to find our camp area in the dark. When the trucks finally discharged their weary, hungry cargo, I led the men to the mess hall and badgered the mess sergeant into getting them something to eat. Too weary myself to eat, I found a cot and fell into an exhausted sleep.

The next morning I received orders twice to have all the men lay out their equipment for inspection. Both times no inspecting officer showed up. When one finally arrived, the men had to lay out their things a third time. Twenty minutes later a second inspecting officer arrived.

"But the men have already been inspected, sir," I said.

"I didn't ask you, Sergeant," he replied coldly, "I gave you an order. Have the men lay out their equipment at once!"

Idiocy compounded stupidity all day long, aggravated by a fall of sleet that turned to heavy rain. I sloshed around through the soggy snow, drenched and red-eyed. Growing more numb by the hour, I seemed to be standing outside myself, watching my weary body obey a confusion of orders like a mindless robot. In a few days the Executive Officer called me to his tent and told me we were pulling out at any moment. He offered me my choice of going to officers' candidate school or going overseas with the company. I chose to go overseas.

We sailed from the Brooklyn Navy Yard under sealed orders, our destination a secret even from our officers. We were part of a convoy escorted by destroyers, the first to leave the United States for the Pacific after Pearl Harbor.

Our troop ship was the S.S. *Mariposa*, a Matson Line cruise ship on the Hawaiian run that had been converted to carry the troops jammed below like sardines. As we eased through the Panama Canal and headed for the Equator, it became impossible to sleep in the stifling troop quarters. Many of us slept on the steel deck, some especially because we would stand a greater chance of surviving if an enemy torpedo tore into the ship's hull at night.

We tried to stay as cool and clean as possible with salt water showers. We laundered clothes by lowering them on ropes into the Pacific, which buffeted the sweat and smell out of them.

One foggy morning we woke up to find ourselves all alone in the Pacific—no convoy, no escort. Our only protection was a single .50-caliber machine gun mounted aft, which any enemy ship or plane would have laughed at. The ship's horn tooted constantly, to signal our whereabouts to the other ships and to prevent a collision with them in the fog.

At midday the fog cleared, but we were still alone, a sitting duck for any Japanese submarines in the area. Many of us were understandably nervous. Suddenly three ships appeared on the horizon, heading in the opposite direction. Two were warships, escorting a freighter. We couldn't see their flags.

Our hearts chilled as the two warships suddenly wheeled sharply and left the freighter, heading straight for us at top speed. As they approached, we could see men ripping tarpaulin off guns amidships. The guns swung around, aimed directly at us.

A man on one destroyer shouted something at our ship through a megaphone. The voice sounded guttural. Were these Japanese or German destroyers? Frightened soldiers in my company took out pocket Bibles, sank to their knees, and prayed. We were all convinced that we were about to be sunk.

Our ship's captain shouted something back, his voice also indecipherable to us. We all held our breath. Then the two destroyers turned, and we followed them. That convinced us that our ships had been captured. We were prisoners of war.

Luckily, there was a different explanation. The destroyers turned out to be British. They were simply escorting us back to our convoy, which we found in another hour or two.

Before our convoy finally arrived at our destination—halfway around the world, in Australia—the blasts of ships' horns sent us swerving sharply several times. Our destroyer escorts rushed about flinging depth charges into the sea around us. Out of an estimated six submarine attacks on our convoy, five enemy submarines were reported sunk.

Our voyage ended in Melbourne on Friday, February 17, 1942, after thirty-seven weary days at sea. An Australian colonel on the dock looked up at us as our ships berthed. Suddenly he took off his digger hat, threw it in the air, sprang a foot off the ground, and thundered out, "Hoorah!"

We couldn't imagine a nicer welcome to Australia.

2
Under Fire

The great gate of islands protecting the north of Australia had been falling to the Japanese. A month before our arrival in Melbourne, the crucial naval base of Rabaul had been captured. Two weeks later the "impregnable" British fortress of Singapore had fallen, giving the Japanese control of both ends of the island gate.

Nine days before our arrival, the Japanese had bombed Darwin, the first such air raid in Australia's history. Invasion of the continent was expected momentarily. Barbed wire was strung around the beaches of Sydney and Melbourne, and a blackout was imposed on the southeastern coastal cities.

The day before we landed, the Japanese captured Java. A week later they invaded New Guinea, capturing the strategic villages of Lae and Salamaua, only three hundred miles from Australian territory. Australians were alarmed when Radio Tokyo announced that the Japanese had also made a landing at Cape York, the northernmost tip of Australia.

The boast proved false, but the Aussies braced to fight for their survival by erecting defenses along a "Brisbane Line." Their plan was to yield the relatively empty and undefendable northern half of the continent to the Japanese, while fighting to protect the southeastern coastal cities of Brisbane, Sydney, Melbourne, and Adelaide, where most Aussies lived.

A week or so after our arrival in Melbourne, wailing sirens sent us running to air raid shelters, although no bombs fell on the city. Meanwhile more Japanese troops poured ashore in New Guinea at Finschhafen, their third base on the huge island.

Early in March 1942 General Douglas MacArthur arrived in Australia to take command of the Allied forces in the Southwest Pacific. He promptly reversed the Australian government's plan to fall back to the Brisbane Line.

"We shall make the fight for Australia in New Guinea," he insisted. A holding operation in the southern half of Australia, he pointed out, would be "fatal to every possibility of ever assuming the offensive." MacArthur was well aware that his own plan was a dangerous gamble. If it failed, Allied hopes of defeating Japan would be seriously damaged. But he felt that only by carrying the war to the Japanese in New Guinea could he throw off balance their campaign to invade Australia.

To launch his grand counteroffensive, MacArthur sought to unify land, air, and sea forces under his own command. But the U.S. Navy's admirals, smarting over their humiliating debacle at Pearl Harbor, were determined to regain prestige by "running the show" in the Pacific.

Admiral Ernest J. King, Chief of Naval Operations, persuaded President Franklin D. Roosevelt that the Pacific war was essentially an ocean operation that belonged under Navy control. The result was an unsatisfactory compromise, with the Southwest Pacific remaining under MacArthur's command, while the Central Pacific command was given to Admiral Chester W. Nimitz.

In the meantime the Japanese Air Force bombed wherever it liked, with almost no Allied resistance. Sixty enemy bombers and fighters attacked Lae, the capital of Australian-governed New Guinea, almost wiping out the native village before capturing it. Enemy air attacks also destroyed Allied outposts in the Solomon Islands, New Britain, and New Ireland.

The last Australian bastion that stood between the Japanese and the conquest of all New Guinea was the tiny garrison of Port Moresby, on the big island's south coast. Japanese bombers flying from Lae began to pound Moresby in heavy raids early in February. Civilians left New Guinea as fast as they could be evacuated. The Aussies now placed the island under military rule.

Our company was sent to a wilderness area twenty-three miles north of Townsville in Queensland on March 19. Before we left I became engaged to a beautiful Australian woman during a whirlwind two-week courtship. We were married three months later in Brisbane.

On March 21 a squadron of American Kittyhawk P-40s piloted by Aussies reached beleaguered Port Moresby to provide a fighter-plane defense against enemy air raids. Aussie antiaircraft gunners had never seen P-40s before. Having just been strafed by Japanese fighter planes,

Townsville, Australia, the author's training area.

they mistook the incoming P-40s for more of the enemy. They shot up four of the Kittyhawks, fortunately not seriously.

The unhappy incident emphasized the urgent need for an aircraft warning company such as ours to track and identify both friendly and enemy aircraft flying around the combat zones.

The ordeal of troops under siege at Moresby, like many events in the war, was not without its humorous side. One Aussie private was loading crates of eggs flown in for his camp—the first fresh eggs Moresby had seen in months. Japanese bombers suddenly appeared overhead and dropped a string of bombs nearby. The infuriated Aussie private shook his fist at the sky.

"You break one of these eggs," he roared, "and I'll come up and break your bloody necks!"

At our wilderness camp near Townsville a rumor went around that Japanese troops had invaded Queensland. I was dispatched at night by jeep to speed through the trackless bush to warn the jungle outpost where one of our radar units was setting up camp. Ordered to be on the lookout for enemy patrols, I rode the running board with my .45 cocked in my hand, as the driver raced through ravines, ponds, and bumpy fields. Our headlights picked out startled dingoes, pheasants, and leaping kangaroos.

I enjoyed the drama and excitement of the wild ride. But I was relieved when the rumor of invasion proved false.

Other rumors about the Japanese proved true. We heard that when diggers—the Aussie term for their troops—were forced to surrender to the enemy, their wrists were tied behind their backs and they were bayonetted to death one at a time. Wounded Australians in tent hospitals were bayonetted on their cots.

At first we were skeptical about these "atrocity stories" as government propaganda, but they were later verified.

At Salamaua airfield, over one hundred natives who had supported the Australian forces were lined up against the wall of a hangar and shot as an object lesson. Many frightened natives, put to work unloading Japanese stores at the port, fled into the bush during the night.

My platoon moved into Townsville to begin training. We knew very little about aircraft warning systems, except for some brief lessons aboard the S.S. *Mariposa*. Now we joined forces with the Aussies to work out joint operations.

Our company consisted of three platoons and a headquarters. Two of the platoons were designated to operate radar units in forward areas close to or within enemy territory. Radar operators picked up and traced all flights within their range on scopes. Information on the planes was radioed or phoned to a Fighter Sector. (Friendly aircraft emitted a special radio signal.) Similar information from visual sightings was transmitted by Aussie spotters hidden in enemy territory.

The Fighter Sector in a combat zone was usually located in a large tent. In its center a large map of the area was painted on connected tables. The map was marked off in grid squares designated by coordinate numbers and letters, so that the location of planes reported by radar units and spotters could be accurately represented.

This map table was manned by the third company platoon—the plotting platoon—around the clock. It provided aircraft warning as quickly as possible of approaching enemy raids on the base. The plotters at the table wore headsets; when they received flight information, they would set up "trees" at the reported map coordinates.

Each tree stand represented a flight, displaying the number of planes, altitude, and a red (enemy), green (friendly), or "U" (unknown) tag at the flight's last reported position. The direction of the flight would be shown by a colored wooden arrow at the base of the tree. New arrows would be added to trace the flight as the plotters received new information.

The controller, usually a combat flying officer, watched all red or U-tagged flights approaching the base. If he suspected a raid, he would scramble the base's fighter planes to intercept the enemy flight. At the same time, the antiaircraft officer present would alert his ack-ack (Army jargon for antiaircraft) batteries defending the base. The controller would order a Red Alert, and a siren would send everyone who did not have to stay at his post rushing to reach a slit trench before bombs started falling.

As master sergeant of the plotting platoon, I was responsible for its operations in the Fighter Sector. I worked with the controller to try to determine which flights were probably enemy; which conflicting reports were most trustworthy; and, when the track of an unidentified or enemy flight was lost, where it probably was at any given moment.

When a Fighter Sector went into operation at a forward air base, if we did our job well, an enemy raid would find our troops safe in slit trenches, our fighter planes attacking the invaders, and our antiaircraft guns pumping hot lead skyward.

If we failed, soldiers were killed on the ground, enemy planes bombed and strafed the base at will, and there was no accurate antiaircraft fire to force the enemy to stay high, making his targets more difficult to hit.

At Townsville two Red Alerts were called when unidentified flights approached, but no bombings occurred. On April 11 we were ordered to Brisbane for further training at the city's Fighter Sector. Unfortunately I was hospitalized with dengue fever.

On May 7 a huge Japanese task force headed south in the Coral Sea. Allied Intelligence was unsure whether its target was Port Moresby or the Australian mainland. Every available Allied plane was ordered to attack the immense fleet from our land bases as U.S. Navy aircraft carriers went into action.

A violent naval and aerial battle raged for two days, with the fate of Australia in the balance. My platoon was turned out at 5:00 A.M. and placed on alert in case the Japanese task force broke through. The conflict was a strange one, in that the opposing fleets never saw each other. They sunk each other's ships by launching dive-bombers from carriers.

Fortunately for us, the enemy suffered losses severe enough to force them to turn back. The U.S. aircraft carrier *Lexington* was sunk during the fierce Coral Sea battle, but Australia was saved—temporarily. No one doubted that an even more awesome attack would soon follow. The last American forces in the Philippines had surrendered, releasing more Japanese sea and air power to strike southward.

As a grim harbinger, Japanese submarines shelled the Aussie cities of Newcastle and Sydney. We were placed on twelve-hour shifts at the Fighter Sector in Brisbane.

On June 7 a second naval clash took place. The Battle of Midway resulted in a major defeat for the enemy, who lost four aircraft carriers and 275 planes.

But the Japanese threat to capture all of New Guinea was still serious. Although their navies had been repulsed, their armies had yet to suffer their first defeat in the war.

General MacArthur was determined to send a task force to Milne Bay, at the southeastern tip of New Guinea, to build an airfield from which American bombers could sink any new convoy headed for Australia.

Meanwhile the Japanese had captured Buna and Gona, south of Lae. They sent a large force up the Kokoda Track, which ran over the wild country of the Owen Stanley Range, to attack Port Moresby and drive the last Aussies out of New Guinea. Australians and Japanese fought each other in grim bayonet battles in the mountain jungles. MacArthur rushed two brigades of the crack Australian 7th Division, infantry veterans of Middle East desert warfare, to Port Moresby.

Confident of victory, the Japanese printed millions of pounds of Australian invasion money. Their bombers pulverized Moresby and the northern Australian port of Darwin. Allied Intelligence reported the organization of great new enemy invasion fleets in the seas above New Guinea.

Only one thing stood in the way of an invasion of the continent Down Under. The Japanese first needed con-

"Diggers" of the Australian 2nd 9th Infantry, who fought in the Middle East before fighting in New Guinea. (Australian Department of Information)

trol of the Coral Sea between New Guinea and Australia. The key to that control was the strategic, undeveloped harbor of Milne Bay, which pointed like a sword toward any fleet heading southwest. Radio Tokyo bluntly warned the handful of Aussies holding Milne Bay to get out before they were slaughtered.

MacArthur sent another brigade of the 7th Division to Milne Bay ahead of some American engineers and my own company. We were a pitifully small force to be thrown in against the powerful Japanese units dug in on

The author's aircraft warning unit, designated "expendable," embarks from Townsville to Milne Bay, New Guinea.

the other side of the Owen Stanley Range. We were told frankly that we were an expendable task force.

On July 16, 1942, we made the trip on a Coral Sea "ferry"—a lumbering freighter that took four days to crawl from Brisbane to Milne Bay. These were still dangerous waters, despite our Coral Sea victory. We wore life jackets throughout the trip. If we had been bombed or torpedoed, however, survival would have been doubtful. We were carrying a large cargo of high explosives and gasoline on deck and in the hold.

Our life rafts were simply two air-filled cylinders bearing an emergency chest, surrounded by two slatted wooden frames. If we were hit, a slashed rope would release two rafts at a time from a slanted device that tipped each pair at the rail.

Our sleeping quarters were in the hatch. Six or seven taut rectangles of canvas made up a tier, and rows of tiers extended from wall to wall. Choice spots were the fifth or sixth slats up, since they offered more air and less dust to breathe. But in any spot it was difficult to turn without hitting soldiers sleeping—or trying to—on every side.

Many soldiers preferred sleeping topside. Slumped in jeeps and trucks that jammed the decks, they slept uncomfortably but coolly. The less lucky simply spread thin blankets on the hard deck. Topside sleepers felt more secure in case of attack. Those who slept in the hatch prudently kept their pants and shoes on.

There were two meager meals a day for the enlisted men, as on the *Mariposa*. Some soldiers made a third out of tinned goods they had bought in Australia. Others waited hopefully outside the crew mess for some buckets of extra food that sympathetic crewmen brought out secretly.

Toward the end of the voyage, crates of spoiled oranges from the officers' mess were placed on the garbage heap aft. Some twenty GIs scrambled to plunder the

The author en route from Australia to New Guinea.

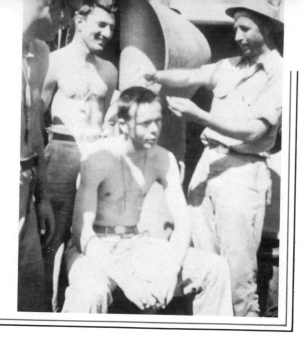

GI barber gives a GI haircut aboard the ship taking troops from Australia to New Guinea.

garbage. Others broke into the ship's stores to purloin oranges for themselves. An appeal urging soldiers not to plunder was broadcast over the ship's public address system.

"My father's taxes paid for those oranges," one juice-stained GI told me. "I'm as entitled as any officer!"

Most of us on the Coral Sea run remained dirty throughout the voyage. Few of us had changes of clothing, and those who did were usually too hot and tired to dig them out of their jumbled barracks bags. Besides, saltwater showers were an ordeal for those who made the effort, because soap wouldn't lather.

Many GIs spent their time at dice or cards, or gambling on "two-up," the national Australian game. Three large Australian pennies were spun into the air by a flat wooden handle, with two heads or two tails deciding the winning bets. Other soldiers preferred to write letters home or indulge in the popular GI pastime of "shooting the breeze"—talking about anything that came to mind.

We arrived at Milne Bay by moonlight to avoid being a sitting duck for enemy bombers, which had already made twenty raids on the base. The huge, beautiful harbor shimmered like corrugated foil. Native fishing boats came out to take us ashore. We descended from the freighter on rope ladders. The native craft swayed perilously under the heavy cargoes of soldiers and barracks bags as they were paddled to two rickety jetties.

Almost as soon as we landed a siren wailed. The siren was activated by the base's only air raid warning system—radioed messages from Aussie spotters concealed farther up the coast to watch enemy flights. We scrambled under the coconut trees fringing the shore for what protection they might afford from flying shrapnel. Soon a few bombs dropped somewhere, and the All Clear sounded.

Waiting for orders, we milled around in the dark—hot, tired, and thirsty. Some soldiers started climbing the

Chow line aboard troop ship taking the author's platoon from Townsville to Milne Bay.

trees to get some coconut milk. Others threw rocks up to knock coconuts out of the trees. One of our men was hit on the head by a falling coconut and required medical treatment.

In the glare of headlights of Australian Army trucks sent to take us to our camp area, some of us struggled to tear the husks off the coconuts. Aussie diggers who had arrived in Milne Bay two weeks earlier warned us against eating the meat or drinking the milk of coconuts lying on the ground. Fermented coconuts could give you a bad case of dysentery.

I asked an Aussie sergeant what Milne Bay was like.

"Mosquitoes, death adders, and crocodiles," he replied cheerfully. "Blackwater fever. But don't worry, mate.

The author risks drinking a fermented coconut—niu rata—the beer of New Guinea.

You'll be too busy ducking the bloody bombs to care much about the rest!"

He told me that the units at the base were one RAAF (Royal Australian Air Force) squadron, flying our P-40 Kittyhawk fighters, and a brigade of the Aussie 7th Infantry. And he warned me not to let "Washing Machine Charlie" keep me up too much.

"That's what we call the bloody buggers that fly over us on clear nights," he explained. "They drop a bomb here and a bomb there, so that our lads have to hit the slit trenches and don't get any sleep."

The Aussie trucks took us on a jolting ride of a few miles to a coconut plantation clearing, where we dismounted and were handed field rations. Some men wolfed theirs down on the spot. Others set up cots in the field and flopped down to an exhausted sleep. Men who had lugged their barracks bags with them instead of leaving them behind to be brought up by trucks dug out blankets and mosquito nets.

Nine men were ordered to set up tents for our officers and carry in the officers' footlockers, field desks, and other gear. Holding a field lantern, the company adjutant personally inspected the tents and snapped out commands to improve the pegging. Some GIs muttered under their breath.

No bombers troubled us any more that night, probably because it began to rain heavily. Mosquitoes materialized by the billions. Sleep was also shattered by the screech of agonized truck motors as heavy wheels spun and slipped on deepening mud.

A few days after we had set up our camp, we had our first real, frightening air raid. The noise was deafening. Enemy planes droned, roared, whined overhead for what seemed like an eternity. There had been no Red Alert. I had been caught walking with some of my men down a muddy road that led to the tent where Fighter Control headquarters was being organized.

Without warning, three Japanese Zeros came flying toward us at treetop level, their guns winking. Instinctively we flung ourselves into a shallow, muddy ditch beside the road.

Machine guns spluttered in the clouds—rumbling, jagged thunder. I felt the ground tremble as Aussie antiaircraft guns pounded away, their thuds sounding like the impact of bombs.

Face down in the ditch, we raw recruits were terrified. This was, after all, the first time in our lives that somebody was trying very hard to kill us, and coming close to succeeding.

We forced ourselves to crack bad jokes, trying to convince each other that we were really cool under attack. But each time the noises of falling bombs crashed closer, we hugged the earth more intensely. None of us dared look up at our attackers.

When the All Clear finally sounded, we gathered in groups, laughing with hysterical relief that we were still among the living. Nearby, soldiers had been lining up for a mess call of field stew. When the attack began, mess kits had been flung away in wild abandon. Some of them lay several yards away, testifying to the speed with which the chow line had dispersed. Dripping soldiers, including the supply sergeant, whose new uniform was solid mud, climbed out of the creek.

That was our baptism of fire.

At 3:00 A.M. there was another Red Alert. GIs poured out of their tents, seeking any natural furrow for partial shelter. Some bombs dropped in the area of the airstrip, half a mile away. Then the All Clear sounded again.

When I returned to my tent, a sergeant who also slept there told me, "Hey, I feel like digging. How about you, Jules? A nice, deep slit trench!"

"At three in the morning?" I yawned. "I think I'd rather be bombed." I collapsed onto my cot.

The sergeant asked another noncom, who readily agreed. I fell asleep to the monotonous thud of pick and shovel.

The next day there were rumors of Japanese convoy movements heading our way. A formation was called. Every man was issued emergency K rations, to be eaten only under orders. We were ordered to dig two-man slit trenches all around the perimeter of the camp area.

Rumors spread like measles. One GI who had a radio reported that he had heard a Japanese woman broadcaster from Rabaul warn troops at Milne Bay to surrender or be cut to pieces.

There was an official report that a large Japanese convoy had been sighted in the Trobriand Islands.

And they were headed directly for Milne Bay.

3
The New Guinea Jungle

The tension was relieved somewhat at evening chow, when each man received an unexpected bottle of Australian beer. Those who didn't drink beer sold theirs to those who did.

Relentless downpours five or six times a day drenched soldiers on camp building projects. GIs who dug slit trenches on level ground were dismayed when the ground became saturated and their refuges filled with rainwater. Wiser soldiers built their trenches on hillsides, with drainage slits.

Mud was king. When we came from the chow line, mud clung to our kneecaps, splashed our hands, splattered our chests. The creek that ran through camp, swollen by heavy rains, washed away the bridge between camp and the mess tent. A rope was stretched from one side to the other and fastened to trees. To avoid being swept away, we had to hold onto the rope while crossing the racing waters.

We who experienced New Guinea thought it the ultimate nightmare country. During the rainy season we battled *gubas*—tropical storms so powerful that the wind-driven rain slashed at us sideways. If we did not take the precaution of clinging to trees, we were often blown over.

The torrents poured down continuously, morning, noon, and night, day after day. We were always soaked. Everything we possessed mildewed. And our terrain was invariably flooded, with much of the ground spongy and muddy.

We tried to keep the clothes not on our backs reasonably dry by improvising bureaus out of fruit boxes. We had to be cautious about reaching into the boxes. Deadly snakes sometimes crawled into our things and would bite a probing hand. Snakes even managed to crawl inside mosquito nets placed over the cots, so we checked our blankets before getting under them.

We were also kept jittery by shots suddenly fired from various parts of the plantation area. We were never sure whether or not these signaled the expected enemy invasion. Usually they represented the attempts of GIs to shoot coconuts out of the trees. I tried it myself once with my .45, but I only managed to ventilate the coconut. Milk poured from the height of the tree. Perspiring GIs took turns standing open-mouthed beneath the white waterfall.

Living under primitive conditions weakened us physically, making us prey to such jungle illnesses as malaria, dengue, jungle rot, dysentery, and scrub typhus. We took quinine regularly to keep from coming down with malaria. Soon after we established our camp, some men began complaining of sore throats. Their temperatures ran to 101 and higher. One or two men collapsed in the chow line. Medics diagnosed the malady as tropical fever, and the men were ordered to their cots for several days.

Turning "jungle-happy," the GI term for weird behavior inspired by the tropics (also known as "troppo"), many soldiers began to sport outlandish beards and strange haircuts. At that time almost every civilian male and stateside serviceman was clean-shaven and had a crewcut. Some beards were goatees; some ran from ear to ear under the chin; some imitated Lincoln's; some blossomed into fierce sideburns like the villainous banker's in an old-time melodrama.

Some GIs sported war-bonnet haircuts that left them bald except for a mane running along the center of their scalp and down their neck. One man cut his hair short,

The Aussies train Papuan natives in mosquito control techniques to fight malaria.

with an enormous "V" for victory traced in baldness. Some adopted Friar Tuck halo haircuts. It was a field day for amateur GI barbers, who used tree stumps for barber chairs.

During our first fortnight in New Guinea there were two more daytime air raids. Crouching against a hillside, I watched a dogfight between a P-40 and a Zero. I could hear the jagged machine-gun fire of the dueling planes overhead. Most of the time my vision was obscured by low-banked clouds. Finally I saw two Zeros plunge through the clouds, smoke pouring from their tails.

The Aussies flying our P-40s were seasoned veterans from the Middle East, daring and skilled fliers. Once two Aussie pilots went up to challenge five Zeros that were flying protection for a flight of enemy bombers. The enemy planes, machineguns chattering, circled, dove, and wheeled with breathtaking speed around the P-40s. Although they were outnumbered, the Aussie pilots refused to turn tail. They twisted and fought for ten tense minutes. One went into a screaming dive to avoid tracer bullets.

"I'd blacked out twice," he later told an Australian war correspondent.:

I couldn't see the controls, but I managed to keep some sort of consciousness by pushing my chin down on my chest and screwing my head round against my left shoulder. The purple screen across my eyes drifted away, and I pulled out of the dive. The Zero came after me. I didn't seem able to get away. And then I saw our other Kitty racing in from the side. He drove right through us between the Zero and my tail, taking every Japanese bullet right down the length of the fuselage. His tail was almost shot away, and the pilot took a bullet in his arm. But he saved me.

How we avoided a triple collision I don't know. The Japanese pilot must have almost pulled the joystick out doing that loop turn to dodge away. But he'd lost the chance of getting me. I knew I had him now. I could see my tracers streaming into the rim of his cockpit. A lick of black smoke squirted out, and he went down ablaze in a flat spin. I looked round for my cobber [mate], but he'd gone. Later I found that he'd shot a Zero down himself and then landed his riddled plane safely. How he got her down with the rudder just hanging in ribbons will always be a mystery to me.

After a while most of us on the ground ignored the air raid siren unless we actually heard or saw enemy planes. There were so many Red Alerts that if we had taken to slit trenches each time the siren wailed, we would never have been able to get our work done. As a result, we were often compelled at the last moment to dive for the nearest trench that had any room.

The reaction of the natives was another reason we resisted taking shelter unless it was absolutely necessary. The ones working in our camp were highly sensitive to our responses. If we remained calm, they felt reassured and continued working. But if we ran for shelter, they would invariably "go bush"—disappear into the jungle. Costly time would be wasted until we could effect their return.

In due time an official order was issued to the whole base. No one was to go to a slit trench on the sounding of a Red Alert; everyone was simply to keep his eyes open for enemy planes.

The order had some unfortunate results. One night the siren wailed three times. Four bleary-eyed GIs sat on the edge of their cots, trying to make up their minds whether to go to their slit trench a third time. A daisy-cutter—a bomb designed to explode shrapnel sidewise at ground level—landed in the middle of their tent. Three men died instantly. The fourth lost an arm and suffered a severe head wound.

The enemy liked to bomb us at noon, when we were lining up for chow. No GI wanted to give up his place on the line for a Red Alert that might turn out to be a false alarm. The result was often a wild, last-minute scramble for slit trenches, with mess kits flying all over the place.

One day the Japanese sent twenty-three of their largest bombers over our base at 10,000 feet. They flew wingtip to wingtip, in a line that stretched across the entire base. It looked as though when they finished with us, there would be nothing much left of Milne Bay. Not much was.

The bombers blew up ammunition dumps, smashed planes on the ground, and hit our food supplies. At the airstrip a truckload of Aussies was waiting to board a DC-3 transport. They stood jammed in the truck, shoulder to shoulder, watching the "big show." The bombers scored an almost direct hit on the truck.

Because the airstrips at our base were too small to accommodate our own bombers, our P-40 fighters had to be used on local bombing missions. Torpedoes strapped to their bellies, they flew out against Japanese shipping that was landing men and supplies along the New Guinea coast north of us.

There was dismay at base headquarters when some torpedoes, instead of speeding ahead toward their targets, simply sank in the sea where they were dropped. An investigation revealed that a money-hungry American sergeant in charge of the torpedoes had been draining some of the alcohol fuel and selling it as liquor. He was court-martialed and given a stiff sentence.

The main dirt road was a headache during the rainy season, which set in on our arrival. No number of engineer crews, toiling naked to the waist, could keep Army

Natives watch a bombing raid in Milne Bay.

vehicles trying to convey supplies from the port from clogging traffic by bogging down in the mud. The U.S. Army's 2½-ton trucks spent more time pulling out mired cars than transporting goods or personnel.

One night I rode a truck that took six hours to travel two miles. Other trucks tried to bypass the jam by going around the road but succeeded only in digging themselves into mud up above their wheels. The vehicle that had caused the traffic jam was finally hauled out of the way into a ditch by three trucks pulling in tandem.

A temporary lull in the rainstorms finally allowed improvements to be made on the unreliable road. New regulations were issued, permitting only "uptown" traffic during certain hours, and "downtown" traffic during intervening hours. Prudent drivers still took canned rations with them on a haul.

Base headquarters decided that our vital aircraft warning operation at the coast was too vulnerable to bombing and invasion. We were ordered to build a Fighter Sector on the jungle mountain that rose behind the base.

I was placed in charge of a native work gang under a head man named Boraki, with three GIs to stand guard. Boraki wore woven bracelets high on his arms, a string of hand-tooled shells around his neck, and a flower and comb in his mass of frizzled hair. Although he was a mission-trained Papuan, his knowledge of English was extremely shaky. I had to make myself understood largely by pidgin English and gestures.

The adjutant warned me to hang on to Boraki, no matter what happened, because we would need him as a guide through the jungle if an enemy invasion compelled us to retreat.

For one night and most of the following day, our expedition slashed its way through the heavy jungle that matted the steep, slippery mountain trail we had to climb. We finally arrived at a narrow plateau commanding a beautiful view of both the bay and the base.

The natives made themselves lean-to shelters against the mountain wall from sago palm fronds. After a rest and some K rations, my men and I slung our jungle hammocks between some trees. Breaking open our toolboxes, we tried to dig slit trenches. But the mountain was almost solid rock, and we soon abandoned the effort.

The natives, expert builders of huts and longhouses, cut trees for lumber to build the Fighter Sector. I made

Boraki understand that only straight trees that were not close together were to be felled. I wanted no clearing to make any Japanese observation plane suspicious.

The GIs with me stood guard against enemy planes and patrols while the Papuans built the Fighter Sector. It was slippery work. The heavy rains had turned what earth there was on the mountain into sliding ponds of mud, and the soldiers could scarcely move around without slipping onto their faces or backs. The barefoot natives, carrying coconut logs on their shoulders—their slender bodies belied an incredible strength—grinned in delight at our ineptitude at coping with mud.

The mouths of almost all the natives were dyed a vivid red, the result of chewing betelnut. This native nut had narcotic qualities, which accounted for the perpetual grins of the Papuans, who moved in a kind of blissful stupor. Yet, surprisingly, the drug never interfered with their capability as workers. How much harm it did their bodies I had no way of knowing.

When the Red Alert sounded down below in the base area, I ignored it to make certain the natives didn't melt away in the jungle, not to be seen again for a week or longer. I assured Boraki in pidgin English that there was nothing to worry about. I promised to stand at our highest elevation as a lookout. Whenever any close danger threatened us from Japanes *eroplani*, I assured him, I would fire my pistol in the air. Then everyone could duck for cover. Meanwhile Boraki and his men should continue to build the Fighter Sector.

One day a Japanese observation plane circled over us, then came back for a second look. Around noon the next day, a formation of about twenty Zeros flying cover for some enemy bombers broke out over the mountains at the usual spot. Two Zeros peeled off and headed in our direction. The others continued on toward the airstrip as our own fighters rose to intercept.

46

As the two enemy planes raced toward us, I grabbed Boraki and said, "Go bush quick with your men—but not far! Jap *eroplani*. They go way, you come back. No be 'fraid!"

"Me no *qari*," he assured me tremulously.

I fired three shots. The natives melted into the shrubbery. My men and I dove off the mountain shelf, seeking niches in the rounded side of the mountain. We felt naked and exposed to the sky. The first plane roared overhead. Machine guns sputtered in the clouds—rumbling, jagged thunder.

The two planes made about four strafing passes each. My cheeks were white and scratched from pressing them so hard against the rocks. The raid was over in about five to ten minutes. It seemed more like five or ten years.

I was relieved afterward when the natives returned. But I could tell that not all of them were happy with Boraki's order. Some wanted him to let them return to their village.

Our weather on the mountain was usually better than the squalls that swept over the base below. When it was pouring down there, we might have only a mild drizzle or just cloudy conditions. But at the same time, our ground was impossibly muddy, made doubly slippery by fallen leaves. It was hard to move around without falling at the sharp incline where we were building the Fighter Sector.

My men and I tried to keep ourselves clean in a mountain stream near our clearing. We survived on K rations and coffee, and the natives prepared a food from sago palms.

As the days passed and the Fighter Sector began to take shape, the GIs with me grew more and more irritable. Tempers were on edge from living in tight confinement under miserable conditions. We slept—or tried to— in our tree-strung hammocks or on the floor of the developing Fighter Sector. I had to break up several fights among my men.

Meanwhile, Japanese marines, having established a base and airfields in the Buna-Gona area, were advancing over the Owen Stanley Range. Fighting was fierce on the narrow Kokoda Track where they clashed with Australian troops from Port Moresby.

They were not enough native porters to carry Aussie food and ammunition on the backbreaking climb up the steep mountain range. Some of the Aussies, carrying loads of up to seventy pounds, needed to lean on staves they made from thick branches. Panting diggers hauled and tugged dismantled twenty-five-pound cannons up the precipitous jungle path. Many men dropped from malaria, hunger, or sheer exhaustion. Drenching rains turned the track into a river of mud.

The desperate Aussie infantry commander radioed a plea to Port Moresby for reinforcements. But there were none. Moresby itself was threatened by invasion. An enemy task force had been sighted at night by an Aussie spotter south of Buna. Seven fifty-foot motor barges loaded with Japanese soldiers were moving down the coast toward either Milne Bay or Port Moresby.

Word came to me by field phone from our camp area below. The company adjutant warned me to caution my men to be on the lookout for enemy patrols. But we were to say nothing to the natives that might alarm them. The Fighter Sector had to be finished in a hurry in case the Japanese invaded Milne Bay.

At dawn the base commander sent up Kittyhawks, bombs strapped to their bellies, to search for the invasion barges.

The Japanese strategy was obvious. They were sending half of a pincers movement south over the Kokoda Track in a direct assault aimed at capturing Port Moresby. The other half of the pincers was their impending invasion of Milne Bay by sea.

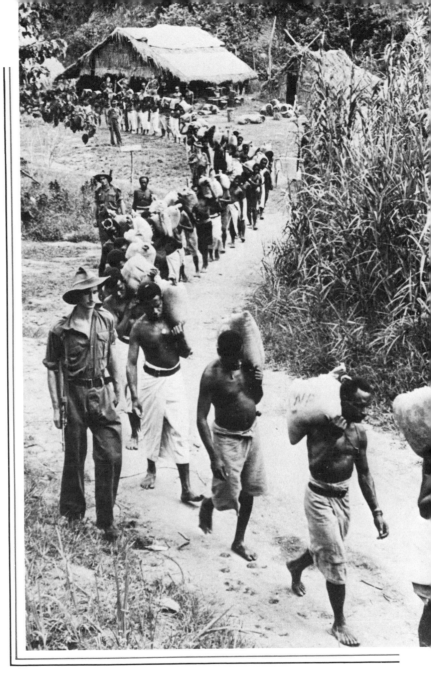

Native carriers set out along the Kokoda Track, bringing supplies to the forward areas. (Australian War Memorial)

49

If the Japanese could squeeze out these last two Allied posts in New Guinea, they would have full control of the sea and air around Australia. The supply lines from the United States could be cut, and the invasion of Australia would begin.

The Aussies fighting on the Kokoda Track were a militia of a bare thousand in action for the first time. Attacking them were six thousand crack Japanese marines. The outnumbered Aussies were forced to give ground before a relentless asault on Kokoda Village, the key to control of the Owen Stanleys.

At our base we still didn't have a single bomber to oppose the invasion of Milne Bay. The Kittyhawks carrying bombs spotted some barges drawn up on the beach of Goodenough Island opposite. Roaring low along the beach, they blew up the barges.

But later that morning an observation plane near Buna reported fresh danger. A large Japanese invasion force, including three cruisers and two transports, was steaming directly toward Milne Bay under heavy low clouds that hid it from our planes.

The convoy was identified by Intelligence as Admiral Gunichi Mikawa's crack Kure No. 5 landing force of marines, who had never yet been successfully opposed.

We were in for it now.

4

The Enemy Invades

Watching from our mountain ridge that afternoon, I saw our bomb-laden P-40s fly out to intercept the invasion force as soon as it came within their flying range. They dove under the clouds at almost mast level to attack, but were driven off by intensive antiaircraft fire from the three cruisers. The invasion fleet landed under cover of darkness.

That night I was awakened by great screaming noises from the harbor below. My heart pounding, I got out of my hammock and saw intense white flashes sear the darkness, emanating from the port. At first I thought they were our guns. But shells of some kind, shrieking high in the heavens, quickly convinced me otherwise. The bombardment came from two enemy cruisers that had sailed into our harbor.

The shelling went on for about an hour, stopped, then resumed. The sound was unlike any I had ever heard. The shells ascended with a deafening, shrill whistle, then arced down with a frightening shriek that grew ever louder as they descended on their targets. Every shell—even those that landed a mile away—sounded exactly as if it were falling directly on our own heads.

My men and I hugged the mountainside, instinctively clawing at the ground as though to dig a shelter with our bare hands.

The natives vanished.

The Japanese cruisers suddenly turned giant blue searchlights on the shipping docked in the bay. Their guns roared and sank a heavily laden freighter. I later learned that port troops worked heroically for twelve hours to get most of the food off the ship before it sank. One staff sergeant was awarded a Silver Star for staying aboard to evacuate the wounded under fire.

Considering the reputation of the Japanese military, I was surprised when the cruisers' blue lights framed a Red Cross ship in port but did not sink it. Subsequently I learned that although some enemy admirals and generals were cruel and unscrupulous, others were humane—it depended on the individual.

The terrifying bombardment went on all night. As dawn dispelled the night, our Kittyhawks once more zoomed up from the airstrip. They rushed with menacing roars toward the position where the Japanese troops were reported to have landed. Joining them were a few B-17 Flying Fortresses and B-25 Martin Marauders—heavy and medium bombers, respectively—flying out of Moresby and northern Australian bases.

The P-40s flew into action at treetop level. I could hear their machine guns snapping as they strafed the landing areas. The bombers sought to hit the invasion fleet. Unfortunately, the weather turned so foul that most of our planes were forced to return to their bases as the enemy forces poured ashore.

The commander of Milne Force rushed to establish base defenses. A company of American engineers set up machine guns at the beach and at the edge of a new airstrip they were building to handle heavy bombers. My field phone rang. The company adjutant explained what was happening. My company was ordered to man gun pits all around the perimeter of our camp, which faced the jungle through which the enemy would be advancing. I was told to stand by for further orders.

The Aussie infantry at the base quickly deployed in strategic positions to resist the invaders. Bad news came fast. The Japanese had landed tanks. We had none. Enemy marines marched behind the tanks, leaping out now and again to try to take Allied machine-gun nests.

One ironically polite Japanese officer would roll his tank up to a tree at night, turn on blinding headlights, and chirp cheerily in English, "Good morning!" Then he would let go with his machine gun. Aussies fired at the powerful tank headlights but were baffled at being unable to smash them. They turned out to be made of some kind of thick gelatin compound rather than glass.

The Japanese thrust was aimed at capturing the airfield so that they could deny its use to our planes and fly their own in. An Australian unit counterattacked in the jungle. I was amazed at the age of the men I saw in uniform. Many were old enough to be the fathers of us GIs. That was because Australia, with a small population, could not have raised an effective fighting force among its young men alone.

The emblem the Aussies wore on the upturned side of their digger hats consisted of a rising ring of bayonets covering the imperial British crown. The symbol was more than picturesque. The kind of fighting in which the Aussies excelled was steel against steel. Apart from cool courage, the trait that distinguished the Aussie infantryman as a superior jungle fighter was his resourcefulness.

I talked to one digger who had been at Rabaul, where 150 Aussies of the 22nd Battalion were attacked by several thousand invading Japanese marines. The cost of storming the beach was 1,500 enemy dead. Incredibly, the Australians suffered only nineteen casualties. They had waited until the enemy overran their positions. Then they coolly turned and ran with the Japanese into the scrub.

"For a few minutes the bloody coots were confused," grinned the Aussie who told me the story, "and didn't know who was who. That gave us enough time to escape into the jungle."

Hunted, the Aussies had split into small groups. Some climbed 4,000-foot ridges, hauling themselves up sheer cliffs by ropes made of tough vines. They had used those vines to swing themselves across deep gorges and crocodile-infested rivers. Constantly soaked for days and weeks by tropical downpours in the wild jungle country, many men dropped with fever. They were carried along on the backs of their comrades.

Many of the Aussies in Rabaul had been captured and bayonetted. But some had escaped at night in launches sent to meet them at secret rendezvous points arranged by radio.

Now at Milne Bay the cruisers returned each night to batter our shore and adjacent hill positions. The tide of battle surged and ebbed over a narrow, palm-fringed strip of land edging the bay. Each night the enemy stabbed and hacked their way toward the edge of the airstrip, and each day the Aussies flung them back.

Meanwhile the American engineers toiled in desperate haste to complete the new airstrip that could bring heavy bombers to our aid.

Drenched by the heavy, continuous downpours, the Aussies who fought the Japanese had to tramp through mud so thick that it pulled the boots off their feet. Some Aussies fought barefoot, wearing nothing more than a pair of ragged khaki shorts. They had to wade across racing streams four feet deep. Roads could not be used, and all provisions, grenades, and ammunition had to be carried by the soldiers themselves.

For eleven miserable days the fighting raged over two square miles of stinking mud. As the enemy advanced, almost invisible in the nightmare jungle, they fortified positions as they passed them. They hid machine-gun pits to cut down Aussies who, charging with fixed bayonets, sought to counterattack.

Hoping to surround the defenders of Milne Bay, some enemy units waded into the sea to attack from the flank, while others pressed through the jungle swamp.

In an attempt to confuse Aussies and Yanks, some Japanese would call out orders in English to stop firing and withdraw, yelling, "It's useless to resist any longer!" This tactic worked once or twice, deceiving some Aussies into falling back along the beach trail. The Aussies dug in at one side of a river, hoping to stop enemy tanks advancing from the other side.

On the second day of the invasion, Japanese planes again filled the sky overhead. From our mountaintop, in a pocket of intermittent sunshine, we watched the Zeros and P-40s whirl around each other in air duels like glinting white gnats. Then the earth shook again with the reverberation of bombs and ack-ack fire, deafening and frightening. We lay prone against the mountain for forty-five minutes.

I watched Kittyhawks flying out again and again to bomb Japanese shipping. Columns of black smoke rose from the distance, and a ball of fire blazed through the smoke. I counted four distinct, separate hits. There was no rest for the exhausted handful of bearded Aussie fighter pilots. Some even threw grenades from the cockpits of ancient Tiger Moth trainers that were used only as observation planes.

"Australian pilots in their squadrons have no superior," observed U.S. Major General George Kenney, World War II Commander-in-Chief of Allied Air Forces in the Southwest Pacific. "I would back them in competition against any other airmen in the world."

At 8:45 that night the enemy cruisers returned to our port to shell us again. Once more I saw tongues of flame leap out of the darkness of the bay. This time the whiz of the shells, and their explosion on impact, was louder and closer. We felt exposed and helpless on the mountaintop.

I had assigned one of my men, a Chicano named Cesare, to rove our perimeter on guard. He was suddenly seized by an Aussie patrol on the mountain. The Aussies were convinced by his appearance and broken English that he was a Japanese spy in American uniform. A number of the enemy wearing Aussie and American uniforms had been caught infiltrating Aussie positions.

Some of the Aussies threatened to shoot Cesare on the spot unless he gave them information on the location and strength of his unit. Only after long and tearful entreaties was he able to persuade them to take him three hundred yards or so through the jungle to our clearing.

I quickly vouched for Cesare, and the Aussies let him go. I decided that he had better be excused from guard duty until our mountain project was finished.

But at dawn I received orders to withdraw from my position with my men. I was to return to camp with the natives, speedily but with caution. I told the working boss, "Boraki, Japanese he come. But you-fella come with me, we take care of you. You go home, maybe Japanese catch you. But my gubmint no let them hurt you. Understand?"

Boraki gave me his betel nut-stained grin. "Yes, *taubada*." But since that was his standard response to anything I said to him I was never sure what he really understood.

Automatic in hand, I led my men down the mountain, the natives following in our rear. When I turned to check on them halfway down, the natives had vanished. We sped down the mountain without encountering any Japanese patrols. I led the way back to camp over several ridges, which were now guarded by machine-gun and rifle pits. It was still dark, before dawn.

"Halt or I shoot!" a quavering voice shouted.

"Hold your fire! It's me—Sergeant Archer!"

Rifles were lowered to let us pass through the outposts.

The company adjutant chewed me out for not having made the natives go down the mountain in front of me so that I could keep an eye on them. "Boraki agreed to come with us," I explained. "How could I know they would go bush on me?"

The adjutant told me that the Japanese were advancing swiftly, seeking to capture the field. Our company had orders to hold our ridge when the enemy reached our position. Every man, regardless of rank, was assigned to a gunpit, and the positions were manned around the clock. To make matters worse—more rain and mud. I hadn't had my shoes or socks off for four days, and my feet were sponges. But I had little reason to complain, in view of the ordeal of the Aussie infantry.

Many of them were fighting barefoot in torn shirts, sleeping only two hours in five days, eating a snack of bully beef and tea once in three days. One Aussie refused to be relieved until every last one of the enemy invaders had been wiped out. A number of front-line Aussies came into our camp for chow.

Many of the enemy, they told us, seemed to be either doped up or drunk on the saki they carried. They came down the jungle path chanting, laughing, and making noise. The Aussies couldn't understand how they managed to bear the ferocious assault of red ants among the coconut trees. Japanese snipers posted in trees would make a curious sound like "Cooey!" which they were under the impression was an Aussie call of friendship. When an unwary Aussie would look up, the sniper would fire his rifle or tommy gun.

At night the enemy kept up a war of nerves. They chattered, laughed fiendishly, and rattled tin cans. They kept working their rifle bolts and firing sudden shots. The inexperienced Yanks were kept on edge. Most of the Aussies merely cocked a bored eyebrow and shot off a round or two to keep the enemy at bay.

Another favorite trick of the enemy was setting off firecrackers. Japanese would throw them from the trees or other concealed positions, hoping that the burst of firecrackers would draw answering fire from the Australians, revealing the latter's positions. They even used a special firecracker bomb that burst in delayed series, to give the impression of machine-gun fire.

Some Japanese troops set up skillfully camouflaged machine-gun or tank ambushes. Others painted their scalps and faces green to blend with the foliage as they infiltrated Aussie lines. One of these would shout, "Forward, men!" in English to trick the Aussies into charging into an ambush.

The value of these tricks soon diminished, however, as word of them spread among our forces.

Japanese tactics were to advance by night and climb into the trees at daybreak. They wore special rubber boots that had a separate space for the big toe to facilitate their climbing. Lashing themselves into the top branches, concealed by foliage, they slept in the trees until dark.

Two Australians reported seeing a Japanese marine climb down a tree and slit the throat of an Aussie soldier who was standing beneath it. Some Japanese would turn over fallen Aussies to make sure they were dead. One Aussie who had played possum reported being turned over but left for dead.

At our camp I took a place in a gun pit on the ridge.

One night I was sure I heard the enemy moving against us at our rear. There were several ways they could have broken through. I had my .45 cocked and on safety in one hand and a tommy gun in the other. As the clanking noise of what was apparently a Japanese tank grew louder, I turned and faced the rear of our pit. I heard laughing and indistinct chattering.

Then I heard a machine-gun burst. Every instinct told me that these were my last moments on earth. What could a handful of green GIs without even a machine gun do against Japanese tanks and crack Japanese marines who had conquered most of Asia?

There was no possibility of retreat or escape. We were cut off on one side by an impassable jungle, on the other side by the sea. We had no alternative but to fight and die.

"You mean there's really no hope?" I had asked the adjutant.

"I won't kid you, Sergeant," he had replied. "We don't have a chance. Even if by some miracle we could beat off

The author, bearded, takes a defensive position behind a coconut palm at Milne Bay.

these Jap marines, there's a big convoy of reinforcements for them heading for us. It will be here in two days. No, we've had it."

As we manned the gun pits, over half the GIs in my outfit had their Bibles out and were praying. None of us doubted that, within an hour or so, we would all be lying dead on the floor of the New Guinea jungle.

My first reactions were panic, fury, grief. It didn't seem fair that I had to die so soon. I was only twenty-six, with so much of life still to experience! I thought of my parents—I was an only son—and what the news of my death would do to them.

But most of all I thought of my lovely Australian wife, with whom I had shared only three months of married life. I felt deep pain at the knowledge that I would never again hold her in my arms. I mourned not only for myself, but for the love I bore her and would never be able to bring her again. If I had had one last wish, it would have been to embrace her once more before I had to die.

But I consoled myself that I had a lot to be thankful for. I'd led a pretty full life—travel in Europe, skiing, whitewater rafting, fine friends, romances. And at least I'd known married life. But I had one more regret, one that rather astonished me. I felt that I would be missing out on one of life's most important experiences—parenthood. I wished that I had been spared long enough to know the love of a child.

That night on the ridge, I wanted nothing more out of life than the precious privilege of continuing to breathe. But, having taken inventory of my feelings, I resigned myself to dying. The panicky sensations I had felt at first disappeared, giving way to a quiet, calm acceptance of death. As the sounds of fighting grew nearer, I said a mental good-bye to the wife I loved, to my parents, and to my friends back home.

The soldier in the trench with me whimpered and sobbed, "Take care of me, Sergeant. I don't want to die!"

"Neither do I, Joe." I told him. "Neither do I. But if there's no help for it, at least let's die on our feet, fighting."

5

The Battle of Milne Bay

We sweated out death for something like a hour. A machine gun rattled somewhere to our left. As I waited tensely, a dark figure stole toward our trench.

"Halt!" I took the safety off my automatic.

"M-m-moontide!" came the stuttered password from the sergeant of the guard. He told me that the clanking noises we heard did not emanate from a Japanese tank, but from an old U.S. Army truck. The laughing and chattering came from Aussies who had come up to relieve us at our posts. The plucky Aussie brigade was fighting desperately to hold off the enemy and their tanks on the other side of the hill.

We weren't going to be killed after all—at least not this moment.

A fresh storm broke. The rain came down in nearly solid sheets, drenching us. The downpour persisted through the morning and continued relentlessly all afternoon. It eased up only long enough for some hot coffee and new K rations to be issued, as the *guba*s swept in again with hurricane force.

Shivering in my trench, as a frightened Joe huddled down miserably in a corner of it, I wondered gloomily just how much more any of us could endure. I felt physically and emotionally drained by the harrowing shelling of the previous night, the lack of sleep, the relentless rain, living in the mud, the soaked clothes and soaked feet. . . .

The unnerving sounds of combat drew steadily closer.

The weather that had protected the Japanese invasion fleet from our planes now became our unexpected ally. When the skies burst open, the downpour turned the base into a quagmire of mud. The enemy tanks bogged down. The Aussies put a number of them out of action by practically diving under their treads to hurl Molotov cocktails (homemade firebombs).

The half-naked Aussies were inspiring figures of courage as they fixed bayonets and charged the enemy marines who accompanied the tanks. In these pitched jungle battles there were heavy casualties on both sides.

Momentarily spared the death I had expected, I found my entire sense of values suddenly changed. Dazed at still being alive, I told myself that I was "officially dead." By all logic I should have been killed that night on the ridge. Since luck had left me alive, how could I possibly ask for anything more than that for the rest of my life? From that time on, I would view whatever joys life had in store for me as "pure gravy."

That realization helped me through the four years I

spent in the Pacific. Whenever things looked dark or bleak, I reminded myself that it was only by a freak chance that I was still alive. That thought remains with me even today, over forty years later. In war, one learns to be eternally grateful for survival, especially without injury.

American bombers, dispatched from Port Moresby, joined our fighter planes in attacking the enemy tanks and planes. It seemed as though all of New Guinea was leaping with the thud of bombs.

When weather permitted, Aussie fighter pilots strafed the tops of coconut palms to topple enemy snipers out of the branches, shot up tanks bogged in the mud, hit supply dumps on the beach, and strafed landing barges.

But most of the time the incessant downpour kept our planes out of the sky. And when the weather did let our pilots fly, Japanese airfields in Buna and Rabaul sent over their own dive-bombers and fighters to attack us.

A series of violent explosions erupted southwest of our position. Ten minutes later an American pickup raced into our camp dragging a Bofer antiaircraft gun. GIs from the fighter control squadron jumped out and set up the gun in the center of our camp. They depressed its muzzle so that it became a cannon and pointed it in the direction of the explosions. As they unloaded boxes of ammunition, one of their officers said that a Japanese force was apparently cutting through the coconut groves on our left flank, heading in our direction.

I posted some of my men behind the bank of a creek facing the grove. Then I splashed through the hip-high, rain-swollen creek, which had become a rapids. My shirt was stuffed with hand grenades, which I handed out to my men posted along the creek. It didn't occur to me until later that if one grenade pin had jostled loose, there would not have been enough left of me to identify as a body.

Everything I owned, including my haversack, was

soaked. I went to a foxhole on the ridge with a .45 and a carbine and squatted down to wait for the enemy. The night was filled with shrill, chilling jungle sounds. We tensed at the approaching roar of gunfire and explosions.

After we waited twenty minutes with our hands ready to pull triggers and grenade pins, the alert was suddenly called off. A sheepish Engineers officer came into camp to explain that some native cows had wandered into a mine field, setting off explosions. The Engineers had promptly shot the rest of the herd to prevent a repetition of the alarm.

The Japanese tried new tactics. Many began wearing Australian and American uniforms they had stripped from dead Allied soldiers. Some wore green-and-brown masks on their faces. A few, masquerading at night in Allied uniforms, tried to stampede units by running into their camps and shouting "orders" to flee because "seven thousand Japs are coming!"

One Aussie unit fell for this trick and demolished its canteen, causing a devastating loss of Australian beer.

Aussies at the front fought tenaciously, sleeping and eating where and when they could. Their courage was magnificent. When they staggered back from the front, dead tired and hungry, the Americans could not refrain from gestures of admiration. We handed over everything we could, and could not, spare—clothing, raincoats, shoes, cigarettes.

We were fascinated by the Aussie grin of courage on every mud-streaked face. To the sweating, exhausted diggers, each new day seemed beyond endurance, yet they continued to endure and fight without complaint. To us they seemed supermen, afraid of nothing. True, many were veterans of Middle East warfare. But even they had never fought in jungles before.

Many Aussies approached battle almost nonchalantly.

One day a corporal from my outfit was driving two Aussie officers toward the front lines when an enemy tank came rumbling toward them. He jammed on the jeep's brakes, and all three men dove into the bushes. They lay there as bullets whizzed first through the windshield of the jeep, then over their heads.

"Guess what those two Aussies were talking about while we were under fire," the corporal told me. "The major was telling the captain how 'utterly frightful' the weather was in Libya!"

The invading Japanese were clever fighters, but far from supermen. Relying on their dubious knowledge of English to confuse our forces, they frequently made mistakes that gave them away. To the traditional challenge "Who goes there?" one Japanese marine called out, "Friend. Good morning!" The guard opened fire. It was the middle of the night.

The Japanese attacked and overran KB Mission, a key Milne Bay position for defending the coconut groves. But they had to leave their tanks, now bogged down in mud, on the far side of the river. They set up machine-gun posts and fired down corridors of palm trees.

On August 28 MacArthur, aware of the significance of Milne Bay to the defense of Port Moresby and the Australian continent, ordered our forces to "clear the north shore of Milne Bay without delay." The next day a Japanese cruiser and nine destroyers headed for Milne Bay, escorting a new convoy of enemy reinforcements. Almost a thousand more Japanese marines landed to reinforce those holding KB Mission.

Fixing bayonets, an Aussie contingent charged the post with bloodcurdling yells. Many were cut down by machine-gun fire, but the rest overran the enemy positions, and retook the mission. The routed Japanese left snipers behind concealed in the trees. A few hours later, at dusk, a force of three hundred enemy troops in close formation

66

counterattacked. As the Aussies fought them off, the snipers opened fire from the Aussies' rear.

Fierce fighting continued all night. Aussie patrols crawled on their bellies through the steaming undergrowth to drag out their wounded to luggers that tried to come up the nearby river. But the luggers were kept off by intense enemy fire. Some diggers from Queensland and Tasmania, lifeguards in civilian life, braved being shot when they swam the wounded out to the luggers.

Some Aussie doctors from the Red Cross ship that had been spared by the Japanese cruisers went ashore to treat the wounded. Working in drenching downpours for a day and a half without sleep, sometimes under fire, standing ankle-deep in mud, they performed critical operations in tents. One South Australian doctor collapsed from exhaustion.

The diggers pushed the enemy back over wretched jungle paths and across swollen rivers. Under heavy sniper fire, the Aussies had to inspect every tree carefully before they could advance. Royal Australian Air Force fliers in Kittyhawks provided air support by strafing enemy positions.

At night some Japanese troops attempted to infiltrate the Aussie units pursuing them. They swam naked along the beach, armed only with knives and bayonets and one sword. Their flank attacks were repulsed, however, and they were killed.

The enemy spearheaded a new all-out attack on the bomber airstrip being rushed to completion. Fighting fanatically, they charged right up to the edge of the airfield, where they set up mortars and machine guns and hurled grenades. The din was so deafening that the GI Engineers manning machine-gun pits had to shout to each other to be heard. Tracer bullets lit up the airstrip, illuminating targets.

67

"The barrels of our machine guns were so hot," Sgt. Paul Marquis of St. Louis said afterward, "they shone like neon light."

Some Americans opened fire from two half-tracks. An Aussie lieutenant got into one to help the busy gunners spot targets. Suddenly he yelled, "Duck!" Grabbing the two gunners by their collars, he jerked them down. Japanese machine-gun bullets flew through the spaces where their heads had been a second before.

All along the strip, GI Engineers and Aussie riflemen lay in the mud, firing across the airfield wherever they saw enemy rifles flash. The Japanese attack lasted three hours. Each time groups of the enemy would charge, Yank and Aussie fire cut them down. Hundreds of Japanese died in heaps, others charged right over their bodies.

Under orders to defend the airstrip at all costs, the defenders held their lines. Aussie mortar crews put several enemy machine-gun nests out of action.

At the height of the fighting, the commanding officer of the Engineers received a message from Port Moresby, asking about the progress in building the bomber airstrip. The High Command, he was told, was anxious to fly in heavy bombers to begin carrying the air war back to the Japanese.

"We are rushing to completion dispersal areas for bombers on No. 1 strip," the Engineering officer replied dryly. "We are having difficulty, however, getting steel matting that was unloaded on No. 3 strip. The Japs have control of the north side of this strip and will not cooperate with us on the southern side."

Just before dawn the frustrated Japanese finally called off their unsuccessful attempt to capture the airstrip. They withdrew into the jungle to wait for reinforcements before renewing the assault. The woods at the end of the strip revealed 150 enemy dead, many of them opposite the two U.S. Engineers half-tracks.

In the bitter fighting at Milne Bay, almost no prisoners were taken. The rule of the jungle was kill or be killed.

Enemy reinforcements once more captured KB Mission. Early in September the Aussies pressed a new attack to retake it. Kittyhawks roared above them to knock Japanese snipers out of the palms. The enemy pretended to withdraw, luring the Aussies into a trap where they were attacked from behind with tanks.

The Kittyhawks again flew to the infantry's rescue, strafing at treetop level. The squadron leader, Peter Turnbull, flew too low. He was killed in his 116th combat action when his wing caught the top of a palm tree.

A Japanese cruiser and eight destroyers entered the port every night to shell the Australian positions, land reinforcements and stores, and evacuate wounded marines.

Kittyhawks carrying bombs took off from the unlighted airstrip in blinding rainstorms to attack the warships. Flying through heavy antiaircraft fire at low level, they managed to hit and sink one enemy destroyer.

Japanese bombers hit the airfield, trying to destroy the American Engineers' defense positions. They succeeded in killing four men and wounded seven.

More enemy reinforcements were rushed to Milne Bay by sea, but now clearer skies gave General Kenney's pilots the chance they needed to sink and turn back Japanese convoys.

As the Aussies strove to rout the remaining enemy forces at Milne Bay, they were held up by bitterly defended Japanese weapon pits. Corporal John French of Queensland was forced to order his section to take cover as three such dugouts poured forth a merciless crossfire. Crawling along in the mud himself, French put the first gun pit out of action by hurling several grenades. He returned for more grenades, then crawled back to wipe out the second one. Unslinging his tommy gun, he charged the third pit firing from the hip.

He got hit and staggered, but he continued charging and firing. His men attacked in his wake. They found all of the enemy dead, with French dead in front of the third gun pit.

He was awarded the Victoria Cross posthumously.

Finally, Admiral Mikawa gave up and sent destroyers at night to evacuate the remnants of his battered invasion force.

In the fourteen-day battle for Milne Bay, one hundred sixty-one Australians were killed in action, as well as a handful of Americans. The cost to the Japanese—invincible until Milne Bay—was over seven hundred dead.

The Aussies had chased the enemy, sought them out, encircled them, wiped them out. "Mopping up" continued for almost a week. Allied fighter and bomber planes completed the job from the air. The victory was so complete that Radio Tokyo honored the Aussies—who already bore the proud designation "the Rats of Tobruk"—by thundering at them as "the butchers of Milne Bay."

The only drawback to the mopping-up was that the Aussies were unable to bury the dead fast enough. In the steaming tropical heat the corpses assaulted the nostrils unbearably, and the Aussies were compelled to use gas masks in order to get the bodies underground.

The last remaining enemy forces were evacuated by sea, under cover of darkness, on the 5th of September.

The enemy had suffered its first decisive land defeat in the Pacific War—a psychological victory of immense proportions that had raised the spirits and hopes of the Allies for the first time since Pearl Harbor. But the Japanese were far from defeated. They still controlled most of New Guinea and the Pacific. There was a long way to go before the prospect of victory could be viewed with any justifiable optimism.

A GI with a grisly enemy souvenir.

Japanese radio broadcasters from Rabaul threatened to send new invasion forces to Milne Bay to wipe us out to the last man, once and for all. We were warned to desert, to get out of New Guinea any way we could, before our bodies became fertilizer for the coconut trees.

With the base secured, the Engineers began building new piers to accommodate the ships we needed to bring in supplies. Wherever we looked, the wreckage left by the battles was visible—the sunk Allied freighter lying on its side, the bomb-twisted Japanese invasion barges, the wrecked enemy tanks, the blasted trees and bomb cra-

71

ters. New U.S. fighter planes—P-39s—flew in to join the Kittyhawks.

Some dry weather followed, ending each day with gorgeous pink-and-blue sunsets. It felt wonderful to be dry again and able to put on clean uniforms.

Abandoning the unfinished Fighter Sector we had been building on the mountain, we opened a new one in a large pyramidal tent close to the airstrip. We got plenty of business as Japanese bombers continued to attack.

We were relieved to be alive, but not too confident that we would stay that way. Intelligence reported a hundred enemy ships massing at the Solomon Islands. We carried weapons when we left our camp to work in the Fighter Sector. Eight six-inch guns with searchlight batteries were set up around the airfield.

On night raids enemy bombers hit fuel dumps, tore up the airstrips, and smashed some planes on the ground. The searchlights, guiding the orange flashes of our antiaircraft guns, failed to bring any of the raiders down. But our defenses were now effective enough at least to keep the enemy from flying too low and striking more devastating blows.

There was much bloody fighting still ahead in New Guinea, battles that were to prove extremely costly to us.

6

Fighting in the Owen Stanley Range

Although the worst was over at Milne Bay, there were still reports of Japanese who, left behind, lived in the jungle, emerging at night to kill where and as they could. Some crept into tents and stabbed sleeping Yanks and Aussies to death. For a long while many of us prudently slept with rifles and revolvers beside us. One sergeant in an adjacent company actually slept with a fully cocked .45 in his hand.

When we ran for our slit trenches during raids, we faced hazards other than bombs. Coconuts rotting in the grove made the ground slippery. Often soldiers would end up lurching into trenches headfirst. Daily air raids continued to kill unwary troops who failed to take shelter in time.

One Aussie, who had had more than his own ration of beer, fell to the ground tipsily beside another soldier and lay beside him as bombs fell close by. During the ten-minute raid he carried on a cheerful conversation, unconcerned that the other soldier didn't reply. When the All Clear sounded, he clapped the silent soldier on the shoulder and chirped, "Wasn't too bloody bad, was it, mate?"

The other man rolled over, lifeless.

When the weather eased a bit, we took advantage of dry days to dam a portion of the stream to make a swimming hole. It was wonderful to escape from the steaming heat and our waterlogged clothes to combine bathing, swimming, and doing laundry.

Unfortunately, we failed to realize that the water was downstream from a native village and was polluted. I was one of the unfortunates who developed a case of what was called jungle rot, a skin infection of spreading pus-filled blisters. Several fellow bathers and I had to be hospitalized for a week.

During one air raid I found myself in a slit trench with the Air Force colonel in charge of the tent Fighter Sector we were operating. The raid was a particularly severe one, with bombs landing very near us. Two other GIs and I cracked jokes, our usual way of dealing with our fear.

The colonel did not share in the repartee. I noticed that he was ashen and trembling uncontrollably. I tried to cover up for him by diverting the other soldiers' attention from his obvious terror. I knew he was a combat pilot, and I thought he was probably suffering from combat fatigue. My guess later proved accurate.

In any event, it was only human to feel frightened by bombs or strafing which at any moment could end your life. One twenty-year-old Virginian in my outfit told me, "Sergeant, I ain't got but one of me. If I lose my body, that's the end of everything as far as I'm concerned. If the world goes on, I won't know it. So, sure I'm nervous in the service. I'd like us to win this war. But with me alive to celebrate when it's over!"

One day the ground began shaking with an intensity I had never experienced before. But there was no enemy in the sky. I suddenly realized we were in an earthquake. The ground was vibrating incredibly. I grabbed for my cot. The cot jumped. I grabbed for the tent pole. The pole jumped. I ran out of the tent and tried to hold fast to a tree. The trees were jumping. So was the horizon.

I thought I was experiencing the end of the world.

After what seemed a century, the violent throbbing of the ground stopped. I collapsed outside the tent in relief. I don't know what the Richter reading on the earthquake was, but I suspect it was one of the highest on record. I have since been in a number of earthquakes, but none approached that experience in New Guinea.

There were often episodes of comic relief that made the ordeal of life in the jungle bearable. One night one of our cooks, who had somehow escaped guard duty before, was finally put on duty on the periphery of our camp. Hearing a noise in the darkness, he immediately challenged, "Halt! Who goes there?" The officer making the rounds replied, "Officer of the Day." After a moment's silence, the cook demanded, "Then what are you doing here in the middle of the night?"

One morning we were awakened by an unusual reveille—hot licks on a saxophone the bugler had managed to obtain somewhere. There were also grins at the base when some Aussie soldiers strolled around wearing a surprise they had brought to New Guinea in their packs—ancient opera hats. The half-naked, ragged dig-

gers wore them with great dignity, tipping them to officers. One top hat later appeared on the head of a proud
village chief, probably a trade-off for some native souvenirs.

The victory at Milne Bay was noted with great satisfaction by all Allied commanders in the Asian theater.
In Burma, Field Marshal Slim told his troops fighting the
Japanese there, "Of all the Allies it was the Australian
soldiers who first broke the spell of the invincibility of
the Japanese Army."

But MacArthur was not inclined to underestimate the
enemy because of one Allied victory. He wrote to General George C. Marshall, U.S. Army Chief of Staff, "The
enemy's defeat at Milne Bay must not be accepted as a
measure of relative fighting capacity of the troops involved."

Although the Milne Bay prong of the enemy campaign to capture New Guinea had been thwarted, the
other one forged ahead over the Kokoda Track in the
Owen Stanley Range. It was led by the Japanese con-
queror of Rabaul, General Tomotore Horii, a small, stout
man with gray hair and spectacles, who sat a well-
groomed white horse with severe dignity. He liked to
campaign at the front.

He and his men pushed Aussie defenders in the Owen
Stanley back toward Port Moresby, which was in danger
of falling. MacArthur urgently cabled Washington for
more forces to blunt the Japanese advance which fore-
shadowed the invasion of Australia.

Fighting continued in the rain forests of the Kokoda
Track through September and October. The Aussies,
outnumbered five to one, slogging along in soaked, mud-
covered uniforms, fought off the enemy bravely. Their
thin, bearded cheeks hollow from hunger and exhaustion, they sometimes spent days in a row without sleep,

existing on meager rations and sometimes yams and taro natives offered from their gardens.

The enemy was concealed by mountain mists that shrouded the jungle when it wasn't pouring. Some Aussies died of knife thrusts without ever seeing their attackers. The Japanese marines, moving soundlessly through the scrub, were expert at camouflaging themselves to blend in with the jungle.

The Japanese finally gave evidence of slowing their advance. It had taken them only five days to push sixty miles from their base in Buna. But it took them almost two months to gain another thirty miles. They lacked supplies and air support because most of their available aircraft were then being used in an attempt to recapture Guadalcanal from the U.S. Marines. And American

The Australian Army's Forestry Unit supplies lumber for all the Army's needs.

bombers were daily pounding the enemy supply base at Buna, smashing Zeros and stores on the ground.

But by September 17 fresh enemy reinforcements reached Ioribaiwi Ridge, in the southern foothills of the Owen Stanleys, only thirty-two miles from Port Moresby. These were crack combat troops of the South Seas Detachment. The fierce thunder of fighting could be heard in the little town of Moresby, now the last outpost defending Australia.

There weren't always enough natives to carry back the wounded. One courageous Aussie infantryman, wounded in both arms, slid down a mountainside, working his way with his feet. "Never thought I'd be crawling away from the Nips," he grinned. When his emergency rations ran out, he went four days without food.

Impatient to break through the Kokoda Track and take Port Moresby, General Horii opened a full-scale attack. The badly outnumbered Aussies fought back desperately, but they were driven out of their defenses and scattered over the sodden mountain jungle 6,500 feet above the sea.

One group of survivors fought their way through Japanese lines for forty days, exhausted on starvation rations and shivering wet during thirty-six days of solid rain, most of them suffering from fever, tropical ulcers, and dysentery.

"This is a thousand times worse than the desert," sighed one Middle East veteran, squeezing the rain out of his digger hat. "Out there you could stay dry, move around and see the enemy. Here you're a bloody sponge. It takes all your energy to move through the muck. And you can't see the bloody Japanese who're shooting at you!"

Forced to withdraw down the Kokoda Trail in a fighting retreat, the Aussies were cut down to less than three worn, exhausted companies. They came down the Moresby side of the mountain range carrying their wounded.

The enemy: a Japanese company fighting in New Guinea.

Australian General Sir Thomas Blamey, commander-in-chief of the Allied land forces in the Southwest Pacific, nevertheless called it a "retreat to victory." Visiting the front, he promised his troops that the Japanese would be beaten by the problems they incurred in their own advance.

"The Japs are already feeling the difficulties of supply," he reported. "They have a few light mountain guns but they have no chance of getting heavy supplies along that terrible track, with its precipices and jagged ridges and awful river crossings and great stretches of track that are merely moving streams of black mud."

The Japanese reached the rocky summit of Ioribaiwa, from which they could look down on Port Moresby. Many of Horii's marines were muddy and bloody, exhausted from the grueling campaign. But now they were delirious with joy that they had scaled the final mountain of the terrible Owen Stanleys and stood on the verge of victory. Some wept with relief.

But they could not immediately advance farther. Horii's plan called for a naval invasion of Moresby at the same time that his men attacked from the mountain. Waiting for the amphibious landing, Horii ordered a badly needed rest for his troops, feeding them with vegetables commandeered from native gardens.

The Australian retreat finally stopped on September 22. Fresh troops began climbing the Kokoda Track to challenge the enemy. The Japanese now dug in hastily to hold their positions.

Reinforced to brigade strength once more, the Aussie infantry climbed the giant slopes, dragging with them dismantled 25-pounder field guns. When these went into action, they blasted huge holes in the enemy's defenses. The troops would then charge these weakened positions with bayonets and grenades.

Meanwhile, Tokyo had learned of MacArthur's plan to attack their key New Guinea stronghold at Buna. Worried, the Japanese High Command ordered Horii to abandon the effort to take Moresby and retreat with his force to help defend Buna.

But his forces were too weary, too short of food and supplies, to withstand the Australian counterattack. Horii had no alternative but to order his troops to fall back.

The stunned enemy abandoned Ioribaiwi Ridge in a fighting retreat back over the Owen Stanleys. Overruning the enemy positions, the Aussies found evidence that many of them had been suffering from wounds, malaria, pneumonia, scrub typhus, dysentery, and hunger. To survive they had been forced to eat poisonous jungle fruits and roots.

"Our casualties are great," a Japanese officer wrote in his diary. "The outcome of the battle is difficult to foresee."

The Aussies fought their way back up toward Kokoda, taking village after village from enemy hands. When they recaptured Kokoda Village on November 2, natives brought them baskets of fruit and decorated them with flowers. The enemy had fled. With Kokoda once more in Aussie hands, Moresby was safe from invasion—and so was Australia.

The Japanese tried to hold back the Australian advance down their side of the Owen Stanleys. Pitched battles were fought at the tiny village of Oivi. Encircling the enemy positions, the Aussies launched an all-out attack. The enemy was forced to retreat in panic across the swollen Kamusi River on log rafts.

General Horii and four of his aides were on one raft that was caught up in the swirl of wild rapids. The raft overturned. The general's aides tried to save him, but they had all they could do to stay afloat in the turbulent waters.

A 25-pounder gun of the 14th Field Regiment, Royal Australian Artillery, being pulled through dense, muddy jungle up the Kokoda Track. (Australian War Memorial)

Australian troops cross the Kamusi River over an improvised bridge built by Aussie engineers. (Australian War Memorial)

"Save yourselves," Horii gasped. "Don't bother with old men." Then he and Colonel Tanaka were swept away, drowned.

The Japanese, having lost 1,200 men in the Owen Stanley campaign, fell back to their defenses in front of

Gona and Buna on the eastern coast. This second enemy defeat at the hands of the Australian infantry encouraged us to feel that we might, miraculously, come out of the New Guinea campaign alive.

Ironically, the American press jumped to the conclusion that it was the U.S. infantry that had prevented the enemy conquest of Port Moresby. Hanson Baldwin, writing in *The New York Times*, declared, "American soldiers were rushed into action and were instrumental in saving the day." Up to that point, however, the only troops engaged in fighting across the Owen Stanleys had been the Aussies.

Typical of the courage that had wrested the Kokoda Track from the enemy was the example of Private Frank Partridge of New South Wales. Despite being shot three times in a single fierce jungle battle, he dashed forward under a burst of enemy fire, picked up a Bren gun from a dead comrade, and challenged the enemy to come out of their bunker and fight.

Rushing the bunker, he found one Japanese left alive and fought him hand to hand. He killed the enemy with a clasp knife. Then, bandaging his own wounds, he refused to be sent to the rear for hospitalization, insisting on remaining with his comrades until everyone in his platoon was relieved.

7

The Jungle Dwellers

When the weather and the war permitted, I occasionally visited native villages, observing what I could of life among the Papuans, our allies against the invading Japanese.

The Papuans are a fascinating people, with tribal beliefs and rituals dating back to the Stone Age. They are Melanesians, a race distinct from the Polynesians who people most of the Pacific. The Papuans practiced ancestor worship, magic, and sorcery, such as the mysterious art of bone-pointing.

They believed that if a native sorcerer pointed a human bone in the direction of someone and murmured the

Papuan natives.

appropriate incantation, that person would sicken and die. There are cases on record where that actually did happen. Psychologists attribute the deaths to a loss of the will to live. The victim, informed that the bone had been pointed at him, became paralyzed with terror and simply accepted death as inevitable.

For thousands of years the Papuans lived in isolation from other peoples and cultures, despite occasional coastal visits from missionaries and traders. Their clans also lived in isolation from each other, resulting in the development of over three hundred different Papuan languages. Communication gradually became possible in the last two or three centuries through the introduction of pidgin English.

Although most tribes fought frequently among themselves, none was so feared as the Sepik warriors of the north. They were headhunters, who also ate the hearts and livers of their enemies in the belief that this added the victims' courage and stamina to their own. They in-

Papuan natives in an outrigger.

spired terror in other Papuans by wearing fierce war costumes—headdresses of cockatoo feathers and necklaces of human or crocodile teeth. They were deadly marksmen with spears. White men who came to New Guinea to trade or to save souls were as careful as the natives to give the Sepik a wide berth.

Most Papuans, however, were a friendly, generous people who laughed easily. Many of the men wore orchids behind their ears. Native costume was usually a blue or red *lap-lap*, consisting of a waistband with a small codpiece for men, and a skirt of grass or printed cotton for women. The men wore dozens of tiny shell earrings through their pierced earlobes, woven bracelets high on their arms, and often a string of hand-tooled shells around their neck.

Most of the natives who worked with us were missionary-trained, unlike their headhunter cousins in the north of the island. When we first arrived, they would scramble up coconut trees and shake down a load of *niu* (coconuts) for the reward of a single cigarette. One smoke was also the price for washing a barracks bag full of soiled clothes. But as GIs bid for their services, they quickly learned to hike up their prices.

Native laborers helped us with our work projects in exchange for Aussie currency, tobacco, or clothing. For the most part, Papuans were loyal to the Australians and willing to work for the Americans, both of whom treated them well.

The fortunes of war cross the paths of Australians and New Guinea natives. (Australian Department of Information)

When any Pacific island natives were unfortunate enough to fall under Japanese rule, they were usually pressed into service as slave labor. Many people captured in Rabaul were sent to New Guinea roped together in the holds of Japanese freighters, then used as carriers for the Japanese infantry.

They received little food and no medical treatment and were "paid" in worthless Japanese invasion currency. Hundreds died of malnutrition, illness, and mistreatment. The native grapevine quickly spread the word that natives anywhere would be best advised to help the Allies, who were humane and friendly.

Of approximately 250,000 natives in New Guinea, some 40,000 had been converted by missionaries and went to church. Many were angels of mercy for Yank and Aussie airmen shot down at sea or over the jungle.

Once a Liberator bombing enemy targets lost two of its four engines to Zero and ack-ack fire. The pilot desperately sought to coax the wounded plane back to base, but when the third motor sputtered and missed, the Liberator crash-landed in the waves. Two of the crew were killed instantly. The other nine hurled themselves into the ocean and swam clear of the wreckage. One of them cried in terror, "Sharks!"

Ominous fins cut curving paths around them in the moonlit sea. The crew thrashed the water frantically with what little strength remained to them. Death seemed inevitable.

Unexpectedly, they heard a soft splashing sound and saw a miracle outlined in the moonlight. It was a native canoe, being paddled swiftly and adroitly toward them by Papuans who had heard the plane go down from their island several miles away. Guided by intuition and their knowledge of the waters, they had located the airmen in the sea.

All nine crewmen were in critical condition, one with a ruptured kidney. For six unbroken hours, a native

The Jolly Rogers crash boat that rescues fliers shot down over the ocean.

Jolly Rogers crash boat GIs demonstrate an air-sea rescue.

gently rubbed his back, easing the pain. Another airman had a broken arm, a third a broken leg. After their wounds were carefully bathed, they were given hot food.

A few natives set out by canoe for a neighboring island where they knew an Allied radar unit was located. A radioed message brought a flying boat to pick up the survivors. The grateful Americans sought to make presents of everything in their pockets to their native saviors. But the islanders would accept nothing. The *taubada*s were their friends.

Papuan carriers who bore the Aussie wounded down the Owen Stanley Range from the fighting at Kokoda won fulsome praise for their superb care. The stretchers were often borne through knee-deep mud in heavy tangles of jungle. Despite exhaustion from carrying their burdens for two solid weeks, the natives always kept two Papuans awake at night to make the wounded comfortable, wash them, attend to their bandages, and feed them.

"These natives," General Blamey declared, "can't be given too much praise."

During the invasion of Milne Bay, the keen eyes and ears of Papuans who worked with ANGAU, the Australian civilian administration, guided Allied soldiers to enemy planes that had been shot down and pointed out enemy snipers hidden in treetops.

Buna natives were frightened into cooperating with the enemy when the Japanese beheaded six of them in front of the whole village and pushed them into graves they had been forced to dig themselves. The terrified onlookers were then ordered to fill in the graves and warned that the same fate would befall any Papuans who refused to obey a Japanese order. Understandably, the enemy was both feared and hated by the islanders.

Most of the structures built for us in Milne Bay were the work of native artisans, who were remarkable

Papuan native riding a turtle. (Australian Department of Information)

craftsmen. Any contractor would envy the way they were able to make their hut walls come out square, and measure off by eye alone the precise lengths of beams required.

One native undertook the construction of a floorboard for an officer's tent. He simply looked at the floor a moment, took his men into the jungle, and came back with a built floor that fitted the tent perfectly. When no tools were available, natives dug post holes with pointed

Native collecting sago palms for thatching a hut roof.

sticks. As they dug they chanted in a native rhythm. It
sounded like *"Whoo-hoo!"* followed by grunts.

Their building materials came from the sago palm, a
multipurpose tree which furnished not only the native's
ruma (hut) but also his clothing, bedding, and food. The
pink heart of the palm was mashed to make a pudding.
Sago leaves were used for both grass skirts and thatched
roofs. The bark was used for flooring, walls, and window
flaps; the trunk, for beams and uprights. Although sago-
palm roofs shrank and leaked after rain, they required
thatching only twice a year.

Papuan building-workers were specialists. Everyone knew his own task and performed it with quiet efficiency. Three or four would weave palm roof shingles. A second group would chop down trees. A third carried the trees back. The fourth built scaffolding. A fifth fastened on shingles. A spacious, well-built native edifice was complete in just a week.

Papuans burdened with thirty-five pound loads had been known to traverse twenty miles of dense jungle in two days. Their slender bodies made their strength and endurance incredible. Living outdoors as they did, they should have been robust specimens of good health. But tropical diseases and the unhealthful climate took their toll.

The cause of most native deaths was malaria. The next most frequent native-killers were pneumonia and dysentery. Another prevalent disease was yaws, a tropical venereal disease that closely resembled the Caucasian's syphilis.

Practically every Papuan suffered from malaria, the gift of the anopheles mosquito. The insects were a source of perpetual infection to us. Very few of us took our daily quinine religiously as we were supposed to, with the result that sooner or later most of us came down with severe chills and fever.

Along with other drugs, the "boss man" of every native work crew carried quinine to hold off the malaria attacks. If a native was too sick for first aid, however, he was sent to the hospital, where he was attended by Papuan doctors.

When the American Army opened field hospitals, many natives preferred to report there for treatment. Although our doctors were not supposed to, they blinked at the rules and took care of the Papuans. For one thing, many natives worked on building the hospital campsites. No Papuan ever wore an honor more proudly than the bandaged arm or leg his friend, the American doctor, fixed for him. He often expressed his gratitude with a woven basket full of exotic jungle fruit.

Once an American doctor had shown concern for an ailing native, he had won a loyal and grateful friend (*tura*) for life.

The Papuans were excellent hunters. One of their popular sports was spearing wild pig. Their spears were six-foot wooden lances with triangular heads and businesslike sets of teeth. They often trapped the pigs and then brought their spears into play.

Because coconuts were a staple food, Papuans learned to climb trees from earliest childhood. Some climbed the tall palms quickly, hand over hand. Others fastened their ankles together with cane and shinnied up slowly with deceptive ease, hugging the tree as they climbed. No one could explain how or why Papuans seemed immune to the vicious stings of New Guinea's red warrior ants, which swarmed at the tops of the trees. The ability of Japanese troops to sleep in the coconut trees despite the ants was equally baffling.

Papuans never touched the abundance of fallen coconuts on the ground, for they were frequently wormy and fermented. Unwary GIs, driven by the heat to assuage their thirst with the fermented juice, were quickly made sadder and wiser by dysentery.

Before the war had reached New Guinea, the natives working on the coconut plantations had gathered the nuts by spearing them on long, sharply pointed sticks, then flipping them into bags they carried. This method was a precaution against snakes (*gaigai*), particularly the tiny death adder which might be coiled beneath a coconut (*niu*), waiting for the unwary hand.

Confirmed smokers, Papuans had graduated from rolling tobacco in leaves to smoking ready-made American cigarettes. At one time all the men had worn beards, but now the ones converted by the missionaries had also adopted the Western habit of shaving daily, using a razor-edged stone. A Papuan beard, in the days of the war, gradually became the sign of a backward native.

Most Papuans were quite modest about their private affairs. Men and women would not bathe together. Frontal nudity was considered immodest only below the waist. They were always careful not to expose themselves.

When a Papuan man courted a woman, he often chewed one special herb and rubbed another around his lips. These herbs were supposed to make him irresistible. Having ascertained that the woman was single and given her the same assurance, he would meet her parents. If the parents approved, the lovers would disappear into the jungle. The following morning, if both were happy about their tryst, they considered themselves married. Converted natives might go through a church ceremony if they were near a mission, but most did not bother. If the tryst was not a happy one, the couple simply parted and went separate ways.

If a Papuan male wanted a divorce, he was permitted to leave his wife and take another. He was required, however, to take care of his first wife and children until she married again. Often she would accompany her ex-husband to the household *(hanua)* where he took up life with his second spouse.

If a husband learned that his wife had been unfaithful, he was expected to rush out immediately to avenge his honor with a club—provided the other man was not bigger or more powerful. Having saved face in this manner, he would then report the matter to the Australian constabulary. The culprit would be fined a pig or similar payment of damages and might be sentenced to a term in the native jail, a guarded village hut.

95

Many natives lived in dire fear *(gari)* of the Japanese, and not without reason. Once some Aussies manning a gun post were asked to search for two Japanese infiltrators known to be near a certain village. They went to the village and asked the natives to join them in the search. In less than ten minutes the entire village was deserted. To the dismay of the Aussies, the natives did not return for a week.

Not all the natives were so *gari*. One Papuan, enraged by the death of his friend at the hands of the Japanese, joined a patrol of Aussies searching out the enemy. Serving as an advance scout, he moved through the jungle with the greatest stealth, so silent that he was able to use his knife to silence three Japanese outpost guards. He proudly wore around his neck special decorations the Australians awarded to brave Papuans.

Natives around our base loved to attend films or other entertainment presented for GIs when the rain and enemy aircraft permitted us to gather in a clearing after supper. We joined each other under lacy palms swaying against the sky like a ballet of fan dancers photographed by a trick lens, a series of sensuous movements captured on one exposure. Low on the horizon, the moon would loom big and yellow over the South Seas.

Some of us would arrange ourselves in a cross-legged arc, as in an amphitheater. Behind the soldiers sitting on the ground were half-circles of Aussies and Yanks seated on gasoline drums, portable tree stumps, and food crates. Behind them, rows of standees. At the rear a GI truck served as a balcony for a thick cluster of soldiers.

Papuans garlanded with red orchids would appear, some smoking American cigarettes, a few of them wearing Australian Army shorts. They lined the flanks of the open-air theater, although half preferred to watch the activities from backstage, whether the show was a film

Natives present a gift to an Army officer at Milne Bay.

or a live Aussie troupe. Giggling incessantly among themselves, they showed betel-red gums.

At one point during a performance, I became aware that every Papuan had suddenly disappeared from the clearing. Two minutes later, the Red Alert sounded, and we all scrambled for the nearest trenches. In another minute or two we could hear the drone of Japanese bombers overhead.

How was it possible for all the natives to know we were about to be bombed a full two minutes before the Red Alert warned the rest of us? We never learned the answer to the mystery.

Some of the natives fell in love with Western sports. At some missions they participated in cricket, soccer, baseball, and football. The Papuans who knew baseball had a peculiar concept of the game. When he was fielding the ball, a native would stick his ungloved hand into the air for the catch rather than his gloved hand. The

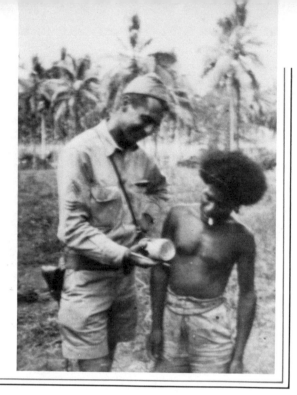

Master Sergeant Archer shows a native a magical product of Western civilization.

pitcher would do his best to hit the batter with the ball. The batter, in turn, would do his best to duck the pitch and run to base. Victory seemed to go to the team whose batters dodged the most pitches.

If the Papuans learned a lot from us, we learned a lot from them. When the war was over, we said *"Bama-huta"* and we never saw them again. But we never forgot the heroic, generous people who rescued and nursed so many of our fighters, who helped make it possible for us to live in the jungle, and whom we could not reward with more than a grateful grin.

8
Disaster at Buna

After the enemy had been forced to retreat from Milne Bay and the Kokoda Track to their bases at Buna and Gona, MacArthur was determined to press his advantage by attacking Buna. Now it was the enemy's turn to go on the defensive. Japanese forces at Buna worked furiously around the clock constructing a chain of underground pillboxes, every one a miniature fortress.

Some were strengthened by sheets of steel or thick walls of concrete. Some were as spacious as 150 square feet. They were protected against Allied gunfire and bombs by fifteen-foot-thick barriers of logs and even whole trees. The logs were held in place by metal stakes, filled between with earth, and camouflaged with jungle foliage. Many dugouts were connected by underground tunnels, so that troops, ammunition, and supplies could be shuttled quickly from one dugout to another. Each was heavily manned, with sufficient food, water, and ammunition to withstand a long siege. And every dugout had machine guns that could lay down sweeping fire in every direction.

To make matters worse for the Allies, the approaches to these impregnable blockhouses were mostly swamps of black mud so deep that a man could drown in them.

MacArthur, unwilling to waste an unnecessary hour of his new advantage, ordered into battle the entire 32nd Division, raw National Guard recruits from the Midwest who had never before heard a shot fired in battle. They were flown from Australia over the Owen Stanley Range to grasslands just south of Buna. This was the first time in history that an army had been airlifted into battle.

But this daring innovation was soon cancelled out by six weeks of trying to inch through jungle swamp in what MacArthur's chief engineer later called "the ultimate nightmare country." The GI's uniforms turned to rags. Their boots became soggy, dilapidated sponges. Staggering from malarias, jungle rot, scrub typhus, dengue, blackwater fever, and "jungle guts" (tropical dysentery), they ran out of medical supplies. Many died in the filthy mud where they dropped.

The bearded, exhausted band subsisted on a third of a C ration and a couple of spoonfuls of rice a day. They stumbled through a world of slippery muck created by the tropical downpours that fell in unending sheets. Bone-tired from pushing through neck-deep swamps, they had no machetes to cut through the vine-choked, steaming jungles. They spent sleepless nights fighting off fierce mosquitoes and swamp rats.

Their camouflaged coveralls of green and brown, which they contemptuously termed "monkey suits," were un-

Caterpillar tractor pulling a trailer loaded with supplies for U.S. troops at Buna. (U. S. National Archives)

bearable in the tropical heat and caused ugly jungle ulcers. The uniforms were also a haven for poisonous ants, ticks, chiggers, and other pests that inflicted agonizing bites. Smokers suffered further because every cigarette in the division, soaked by the storms, had disintegrated.

MacArthur's plan called for two regiments of the 32nd to attack Buna, while the seasoned Aussie 7th Division drove on toward the equally fortified seaport of Gona, several miles west. But Major General Edwin Harding, commander of the 32nd, did not even have the full strength of his two frazzled regiments. He had been ordered to lend two of his six battalions to the Aussies on his flank.

To make the situation still worse, Harding's men were miserably equipped. His engineers had little more than their bare hands to work with. What little radio equipment the outfit had didn't work. There wasn't a carbine in the division. They had no oil and little ammunition for their rusting weapons. Rain, muck, and dirt jammed their mortars, machine guns, tommy guns, BARs, and M-1s. For artillery support they had only two 3.7 howitzers, and the promise of four 25-pounder artillery guns which hadn't arrived. They had no air support because steady rain grounded Allied planes.

Nevertheless, MacArthur demanded a swift victory. General Harding himself, misinformed by MacArthur's intelligence unit, originally believed that Buna would be "easy pickings" because, he was told, it was defended by only "a shell of sacrifice troops." He and his men quickly learned otherwise.

On November 21, 1942, Harding received a radio message from MacArthur that ordered: TAKE BUNA TODAY AT ALL COSTS.

The footsloggers of the 32nd reached the outer defenses of Buna on their approach march without meeting a single Japanese. By this time, however, they were so enfeebled by exhaustion, disease, and hunger that they warranted evacuation. But their officers, misled by the faulty intelligence from MacArthur's headquarters, assured them that Buna was only lightly held. Cleaning out the enemy in the area, they were told, would be easy.

Awaiting them at Buna were nearly three thousand tough enemy troops, dug in solidly and prepared to fight to the bitter end with the desperation of seasoned veterans who had nowhere to retreat and no hope of evacuation. Their redoubts, heavily manned and gunned, were strategically placed to command sweeping firepower against every possible avenue of approach, whether by sea or through the deep swamp ooze. The forts were so thick that they could withstand direct hits from 25-pounders, and even aerial bombings could not put them out of action.

When the 32nd pressed its first attack on the enemy outposts at Buna, they were stunned as Japanese firepower mercilessly cut them down. The clever camouflaging of the enemy forts forced the GIs to fight blind. Enemy weapons gave off no flash, adding to the difficulty of locating their positions. To confuse the green American troops further, the Japanese would shuttle their automatic weapons from one hidden position to another, giving the GIs the impression that they were under automatic fire from every side. Enemy snipers were everywhere, many of them on camouflaged platforms near the tops of coconut palms.

American casualties mounted rapidly. The enemy would let GIs advance to almost four feet of a camouflaged position before opening deadly fire. Sometimes they let troops pass, then mowed them down from behind. Led to expect an easy victory at Buna, the dazed and shaken 32nd fell back in confusion.

They desperately dug foxholes, in which they were pinned down by murderous crossfire. The foxholes immediately filled with rain, but the GIs burrowed into them anyhow. More than half their ammunition had already been expended.

Their only stroke of good luck was that Colonel Hiroshi Yamamoto, in charge of the Buna defense, did not then decide to completely wipe out the Yanks with a full-scale counterattack. Fighting raged for a fortnight. Cut to ribbons, the Americans hardly dared move during daylight hours.

General Harding urgently called for more ammunition and for an aerial pounding of enemy positions. On the first dry day new ammunition was dropped to them by air. Aussie Beaufighters and our P-40s strafed the target area, followed by A-20s and B-25s which dumped bomb loads on the Japanese forts. But the enemy in the thickly protected bunkers, and the bunkers themselves, were virtually unscathed by the air assault.

Once more the weary men of the 32nd were ordered to mount an attack. They staggered forward against the same impenetrable wall of flying steel. In addition, Japanese fighter planes from Lae strafed them and dropped ground-skimming daisy-cutters.

Once in a while a GI was able to survive enemy firepower long enough to get close to a bunker's firing slit and push in a hand grenade. But only a few were successful; most of those who tried it died in the attempt. Later, at Guadalcanal, U.S. Marines burned Japanese out of such dugouts by using flamethrowers. But the 32nd had no such weapons, nor tanks, to help them take the bunkers.

Even their air support proved disastrous. One B-25 accidentally dropped its bombs squarely in the midst of two companies of the 32nd. Six men were killed, another dozen wounded, and some seventy GIs were stunned by the blast. The regiment's morale was shattered.

Now Colonel Yamamoto ordered a counterattack. Screaming enemy troops hurtled fiercely out of their bunkers. Demoralized, exhausted and sick, many GIs fled.

After twenty-two days of continuous fighting against impossible odds and under hellish conditions, half of the battered remnants of the 32nd were finally relieved. Most were in such bad shape that they could hardly stand up.

Despite their bitter loss, many men of the 32nd had performed acts of great heroism. Only later were they rewarded by a shower of decorations, many of them posthumously. But at the time there was no evading the fact that the 32nd had failed in the impossible mission MacArthur had assigned to them in his first offensive of the Pacific war.

Back in a luxurious residence in Port Moresby, MacArthur was furious. The Australian general in charge of Allied land forces under MacArthur, Sir Thomas Blamey, bluntly disparaged the 32nd's performance in battle. Their failure stung MacArthur all the more because of the sharp contrast with the Aussie fighting ability demonstrated at Milne Bay and on the Kokoda Track. He fumed over the 32nd's fiasco as a personal insult and embarrassment to him.

He summoned from Australia Lt. Gen. Robert L. Eichelberger, a tall, thin infantryman. Eichelberger found the commander-in-chief pacing his wide veranda, looking grim and intense. MacArthur told the tough infantry officer that Colonel Harding had failed in his mission and would have to be replaced. All the Buna offensive needed, MacArthur insisted, was aggressive leadership.

"I know that the 32nd hadn't been trained for jungle operations," he told Eichelberger. "I know that they're sick and that the climate is wearing them down. But a *real* leader could take these same men and capture Buna."

Eichelberger was ordered to relieve Harding and his

staff. "You're to do the job," he added, "or I will relieve them myself—and you, too!" He warned that time was of the essence, because the Japanese might land reinforcements any night. Then, continuing his restless pacing, he snapped, "Go out there, Bob, and take Buna—*or don't come back alive!*"

He nodded toward Brigadier General Clovis E. Byers, who had accompanied Eichelberger to Port Moresby. "And that goes for your chief of staff, Clovis, too!"

In the morning, feeling calmer and perhaps a little abashed by his strong language of the night before, MacArthur told Eichelberger, "Take good care of yourself, Bob, because you'll be of no use dead. There'll be a decoration for you, incidentally, if you take Buna. But remember, I must have Buna—*regardless of casualties!*"

Eichelberger did not forget the way he had been given this order. There was no doubt that MacArthur expected him to take Buna even if every man of the 32nd was killed in the attack. The conversation was confirmed when Eichelberger flew to Dobodura to take command of the fighting. General Harding noted in his diary, "MacArthur had told Eichelberger that he was to take Buna or die before it."

In their first meeting, Eichelberger asked Harding what changes the latter proposed to make in his staff to get things moving. Harding snapped angrily that he would replace no one.

"My commanders deserve to be decorated, not relieved!"

Eichelberger decided to make an inspection tour of the front, which was now less than three hundred yards from Buna village. At terrible cost the 32nd had advanced with the help of some new 25-pounders and 60-mm and 81-mm mortars. Colonel John W. Mott, General Harding's chief of staff, was in personal command of operations at the front. Time and again he threw his battered troops against the enemy defenses. Each time the GIs staggered to attack, they were cut down and driven back by withering bands of fire across every axis of approach.

After the enemy had smashed Company E's fifth attack, Colonel Mott wrote in the journal of the 2nd Battalion, 126th Infantry, "The troops that we have left are weak and tired, and need rest and reinforcement." The men were in such pitiable condition that Major Roger O. Egeberg, a visiting medical officer, reported to Eichelberger that they looked like "Christ off the cross."

But MacArthur's orders were still blistering Eichelberger's ears. He grew incensed when he found some unwounded men who had been sent to a first-aid station behind the front to recover from dengue fever, exhaustion, and combat fatigue.

Proceeding to the momentarily quiet front, Eichelberger questioned three machine gunners. They told him that an enemy machine-gun pit lay immediately ahead. It had opened fire earlier on GIs who had tried to advance. Eichelberger offered to decorate the man who would go forward fifty yards to find out if the enemy gun was still there. None of the gunners, nor any other troops, volunteered. Eichelberger fumed.

He was further irked to discover that the unit's officers had not permitted hungry front-line troops to cook some captured Japanese rice. He didn't learn until later what the men of the 32nd knew—that fires made with wet jungle wood raised dense clouds of telltale smoke that served as targets for enemy fire.

A furious scene took place at Colonel Mott's command post. In General Harding's presence. Eichelberger tongue-lashed Mott for poor direction at the front. He snapped that he wasn't even sure the 32nd had ever really fought. Colonel Mott lost his temper and defended his men hotly.

"You're licked!" Eichelberger flared back. He accused the men of the 32nd of having done a "rotten job," and the officers of having been guilty of "coddling cowards."

"Eichelberger showed no appreciation of what the men had been through," General Harding wrote in his diary, "or the spirit shown by most of them in carrying on despite heavy casualties, the roughest kind of opposition, and the most trying conditions."

Referring to Mott's angry reply to Eichelberger, Harding added, "I approved of every word he said and of the vehemence with which he stated his case."

On December 2 Harding was relieved of his command. So were Mott and other staff officers. From now on the show was to be Eichelberger's, and it would be run the way MacArthur demanded—seeking a swift victory, regardless of the cost in lives.

Shortly afterward a lugger carrying General Harding was strafed and sunk by Zeros, but Harding swam two miles to shore and survived.

Eichelberger promptly ordered an all-out frontal attack on the enemy fortresses at Buna. One of his staff officers, Col. Clarence A. Martin, took charge of a front-line position. Martin found that the troops had a prevailing "lack of almost everything with which to operate." Nevertheless, he ordered the officers to stop sympathizing with the troops. That, he said sharply, only encouraged them in their "feeling-sorry-for-ourselves" attitude. Then he dropped his bombshell.

There would be no relief for what was left of the battered 32nd Division until "after Buna was taken." Martin reported to headquarters that he knew this news would come as a shock to the men of the 32nd. "But I was certain," he declared, "that after the shock was over, the troops, knowing their task, would fight better than those just hanging on and continually looking over their shoulders for relief."

Another of Eichelberger's officers, Col. John E. Grose, was stunned when a front-line company under his command was ordered by Eichelberger to make a fresh frontal attack on Buna. Company F was the last reserve. Companies E and G had just been beaten back with heavy casualties. Grose tried to persuade Eichelberger that there was nothing to be gained by rushing a new attack, which called for several days' careful operations.

Eichelberger refused to listen. MacArthur wanted Buna village captured that very day.

Eighty GIs charged the enemy defenses. Within minutes eight lay on the ground dead, thirty-six were wounded, and the rest were driven back in a hail of steel. The bitter troops who survived labeled Eichelberger "the butcher of Buna," unaware that he was acting on MacArthur's orders to take Buna regardless of the cost.

Ironically, it was not one of Eichelberger's officers who became the hero of Buna, but one of the 32nd's own sergeants, a thirty-seven-year-old black-bearded professional soldier named Herman J. Bottcher. The German-born Bottcher had fought with the International Brigade against Gen. Francisco Franco's fascist forces in Spain's civil war six years earlier. The International Brigade had promoted him from private to captain.

In World War II Bottcher wasn't fighting for General MacArthur. He was waging a fierce, personal war against the Axis powers, whom he hated with all his heart.

When his men were thrown back by the enemy in the senseless frontal assault on the 5th of December, Bottcher became bitter at the sight of his officers sitting on the ground studying maps. He glared at them as he filled a bucket of water to take up front to his wounded men.

"If you guys would get off your tails and start fighting," he snarled at the startled officers, "maybe we'd get something done!" Bottcher decided to do something himself. He called for volunteers to drive a wedge into the Japanese flank and push through onto the beach. With a dozen picked men, he squirmed through the swamp and coconut palms, then dashed through a hail of enemy fire. Firing tommy guns and hurling grenades, they toppled enemy snipers out of the trees and silenced several Japanese machine-gun posts. After several hours of heavy fighting, they broke through to the beach and dug in.

At dawn the enemy attacked them from both flanks. Bottcher repulsed the attacks with sweeping machine-gun fire. With the aid of his riflemen, he piled the beach on both sides with forty enemy dead and wounded another dozen.

A Japanese machine-gun crew was advanced to blast Bottcher and his men off the beach. Bottcher crawled out with a pocketful of grenades and blew the enemy post to bits.

For seven days Bottcher and his men fought off attack after attack, an incredible feat. They crawled out of their posts to drag back abandoned enemy machine guns and ammunition.

Bottcher was wounded twice, but he kept on fighting. General Eichelberger himself crawled out to the beach to congratulate the fiery sergeant, award him the Distinguished Service Cross, and inform him that he had won a field promotion to captain.

Before Bottcher and his valiant dozen volunteers were relieved, they had killed 120 of the enemy. Because of the beachhead he had established and held, the rest of the 32nd was able to spear through to the beach. They drove a wedge that divided the Japanese forces at Buna in half.

Bottcher, who was subsequently promoted to major, was killed in combat. "He was one of the best Americans I have ever known," Eichelberger declared of the man whom the State Department had refused citizenship because he had fought for democracy in Spain before it was fashionable to be antifascist.

9
"The Toughest Fighting in the World"

The battle for Buna flamed to new proportions as the Japanese hastily brought in heavy reinforcements by sea, and a new infantry division arrived from the States.

"The Japanese soldier is no easy enemy," MacArthur warned the new arrivals. "He is a hard fighter, and one who fights courageously and intelligently. He gives no quarter. He asks for no quarter. . . . The Japanese soldier has an extraordinary capacity to fight on to the end. He never stops. He believes that if he surrenders his enemy will kill him or that . . . he will be executed when he returns to Japan."

MacArthur implied criticism of the 32nd when he told

the newcomers what he expected of GIs sent in against the enemy: "If, when you are hard pressed, you begin to look for a position in the rear, or begin to think it beyond human endurance to continue the fight, you will not only be destroyed physically but you will lose your reputation in the eyes of your friends and your country. . . . Always the fellow wins who fights to the end, whose nerves don't go back on him, who never thinks of anything but the will to victory. That's what I want of you men—and that's what I expect."

Eichelberger had better success than Harding in getting the support the 32nd needed—tanks, artillery, and the extra regiment Harding had been promised but never received.

Allied air support finally began to make itself felt. For eight hours at a time, the target area became an inferno of flame, smoke, dust, and flying metal as bombs, mortars, and artillery shells crashed into it. But so impregnable were the Japanese forts and pillboxes that even after the bombardment, when the 32nd charged, they found the enemy still alive in their strongholds, fighting as fiercely as ever. Each steel-roofed, concrete dugout had to be taken in a separate, bitter battle.

Even when the forts were overrun, the enemy sought to strangle and knife its attackers or bash them senseless with rocks. The assault was a costly, tedious process.

There was no end to the personal misery of the men of the 32nd. Col. Clarence A. Martin, who later became a general, described it:

The positions occupied became unbearably hot in the daytime as the tropical sun broiled down. The grass shut off all air. . . . Due to enemy observation, any daylight movement among the forward positions had to be by crawling, which added to the misery from the heat. There

112

Australian-manned General Stuart tanks attack Japanese pillboxes at Buna. (Australian War Memorial)

were cases of heat exhaustion daily, and some of the company commanders strongly urged the battalion commander to permit the troops to withdraw about 300 yards in daytime to positions where there was shade, and reoccupy the forward positions at night.

But Martin, with Eichelberger cracking the whip behind him, and MacArthur behind Eichelberger, refused these requests. Martin later explained that he felt such withdrawals would be "psychologically bad" for the troops and "would hurt the rebuilding of their offensive spirit."

Many GIs in the Buna campaign ate cold rations—if they were lucky enough to have them—for forty-five days straight. When some of them finally could get hot C rations, they became ill because they were unaccustomed to hot meals.

In the often chilly, rainy nights, GIs sought to warm themselves with hot coffee. They rigged ponchos over their foxholes to keep out the rain and hide the flame. For fuel they poured gun oil into empty C-ration cans. They would add a few gun patches and let them soak in the oil before lighting it to boil the coffee. Some GIs used captured sticks of dynamite as fuel, crumbling part of a stick and lighting it.

The enemy used all kinds of subtle tricks to confuse the weary men of the 32nd. When Allied tanks landed at the beachhead and hit the first line of bunkers, the enemy pulled back to their second bunker line. Then, when the tanks rolled on, the Japanese infiltrated back to their first line in time to pour a merciless stream of fire on the infantry trudging in the wake of the tanks.

The Japanese fought with fanatical determination beside their own dead. The prevailing winds, carrying the stench of unburied enemy bodies into the nostrils of GIs, created a serious morale problem. The air was so nauseating that the Japanese themselves had to wear gas masks most of the time.

The Australian troops simultaneously attacking Gona were not unaware of the difficulties their American allies were facing at Buna. *Pacific Victory*, the official Australian history of the New Guinea campaign, acknowledged, "If hardened Australian veterans found the going extremely severe, it is easy to understand the reactions of those men from Wisconsin, Oregon, and Washington, dumped into this maze of swamp and jungle, drenched by night and scorched by day."

One Australian commander observed, "Those kids are doing a good job. They are green and inexperienced, and this is the first fight they have ever been in. Doubt if a tougher baptism by fire could be imagined. But they are learning fast, because they want to learn, and they aren't afraid to ask the advice of my troops, who have learned all the lessons at bitter cost."

He added, "I think these boys expected a swift and easy capture of Buna. I was more cautious, but it's a tougher proposition than even I'd expected. These Americans are coming through the test well, and should be great jungle fighters when it's over."

George H. Johnson, a highly respected Aussie war correspondent, took notice of the raw troops MacArthur had thrown against the tough enemy troops who had been seasoned in amphibious operations and jungle warfare:

> When you see these young Americans moving up toward the shattering noise of the front line, or coming back wounded, or sick with the strange jungle fever that is not malaria, nor scrub typhus, nor dengue, you are immediately amazed at how young they look. Many of them look like kids out of high school. I suppose our own troops looked as young when they went abroad [to the Middle East] three years ago.

The Aussies mounted attacks on nearby Gona from two directions. General Blamey warned MacArthur, "Don't delude yourself into thinking the Japs are going to give up this north coast without a very desperate fight. And it will be just as tough or tougher when we clean the whole coast up because, even then, they aren't going to leave us alone."

MacArthur, clad in a pink-silk dressing gown with a black dragon on the back, listened without conviction. He

A dead Japanese marine in front of a smashed pillbox at Giropi Point. (Australian War Memorial)

still believed in his road to victory: "We must attack, attack, attack!"

At Gona the enemy cut down the grass all around their positions to compel the Aussies to run an open gauntlet to attack the forts. An Aussie bayonet charge on one post left two-thirds of their men casualties, although the post was captured and thirty-one of the enemy were killed.

The Aussies frequently gave bloodcurdling yells as they charged the enemy with fixed bayonets. In turn, some enemy officers screamed in Japanese as they charged back waving samurai swords.

"It was the wildest, maddest, bloodiest fighting I have ever seen," said an Aussie private who fought at Gona. "A bayonet charge like that is a pretty terrible business when you see your cobbers falling, when you can only see a tree ahead of you. You can't even see the Japanese hidden among the roots until you're right on top of them, and they are still firing and yelling as you plunge your bayonet down. But it's the only way to clean them out."

Aussies and Japanese battled across a no-man's-land only fifty yards wide, and sometimes were reduced to trying to choke each other with bare hands. The Aussie artillery could not fire freely for fear of shelling their own troops. But Japanese Zeros and dive-bombers, who considered their troops safe in the dugouts, attacked the Allied forces. They also strafed and bombed a tent hospital which was clearly marked on top with a large red cross.

Hardly any prisoners were taken by either side. The Japanese, convinced their choice was either victory or death, fought fanatically. Any wounded Aussies they encountered were killed in cold blood.

"The enemy has brought warfare back to the primeval," General Blamey told his troops grimly. "He fights by the jungle rule of tooth and claw. Kill him or he will kill you."

By December 10 the Australians had captured and fought past all but one formidable Japanese post in Gona. Here they mounted a great mortar barrage followed by intense artillery bombardment. American bombers joined in the attack, dropping loads of high explosives on the position.

This thunderous assault was finally too much for the last enemy defenders. That night, as the inevitable rain fell, the Japanese crawled from their outpost to the beach and formed ranks to withdraw down the coast to Sanananda. The Aussies, who had held their fire until then,

Japanese troops wounded at Gona receive medical care from the Aussies. (Australian War Memorial)

opened up with machine guns as their infantry charged with bayonets and grenades.

When the sun came up, about one hundred dead Japanese lay sprawled on the beach. Four badly wounded men were taken prisoner. Certain they were going to be killed, they were amazed when Aussie doctors treated their wounds.

The Aussies mopped up the rest of Gona, cleaning out isolated enemy foxholes. Now it was up to the Americans to take their still difficult objective: Buna.

The news from Gona inspired the war-weary GIs in front of Buna village to fresh efforts. Cheering wildly, the men of the 32nd smashed along the east bank of Buna Creek and stormed five pillboxes, taking them at bayonet point despite heavy losses. But this victory, heartening though it was, advanced the front only fifty yards in that crowded salient.

It became increasingly clear that MacArthur was playing his perilous chess game with men who could barely stand up. Accordingly, a fresh Australian brigade, brought by sea from Milne Bay in mid-December, pushed past the 32nd's positions. Supported by light tanks, they launched a successful attack.

On December 28 Colonel Grose took the 3rd Battalion out of the line for a long-overdue rest. But General Eichelberger had different ideas. Without even consulting Grose, he ordered the relieved men back into action for an immediate attack on Buna Mission. Grose was so stunned by this sudden order committing an exhausted battalion to such an attack that he could hardly concentrate on planning battle strategy.

Yet Eichelberger, although he was compelled to follow MacArthur's orders, was not blind to the injustice being done to the battered 32nd. At the height of the Battle of Buna, he told the men of the division that when he'd taken over its command, he hadn't realized "what they were up against." After examining captured Japanese bunkers, Eichelberger admitted, "It is easy to see how they held us off so long."

Colonel Grose, even more emphatic about the mistreatment of the 32nd, wrote of the 3rd Battalion, "The battalion's men have been courageous and willing, but they have been pushed beyond the limit of human endurance."

Still impatient, MacArthur sent word to Eichelberger, "Our time is strictly limited. If results are not achieved shortly, the whole picture may radically change." Eichelberger replied that he was throwing into the front line all the fighting strength under his command.

GIs stormed desperately from one underground enemy post to another, taking them in hand-to-hand fighting at terrible cost. The Japanese resisted bitterly to the last, standing on the corpses in the pits as if they were stepladders.

Word reached the Japanese officers at Buna that the Emperor was impatient over the reverses his forces were meeting in New Guinea. One officer snapped, "The big shots in Tokyo should come out here and see what we have to take, and then they might understand!"

At last the heavy sacrifices of the 32nd Division yielded victory. On December 28, 1942, Buna fell.

But the ordeal of the 32nd was still not over. Between the captured enemy strongholds of Buna and Gona lay the seaport of Sanananda, which had yet to be taken. Again Eichelberger threw in American troops without regard for losses.

In one day's fighting at Sanananda the 18th Brigade lost 142 men—34 killed, 66 wounded, 42 missing—whereas the enemy line remained undented. Eichelberger sent a chagrined message to MacArthur: "The at-

General Sir Thomas Blamey and Lt. General Robert Eichelberger at the entrance to a Japanese pillbox complex during a tour of the battlefields. (Australian War Memorial)

tack on that darned area was not successful. The advance went through where there were no Japanese, and bogged down where the Japanese were."

At this late date it began to dawn on Eichelberger that there were ways of winning a victory against the Japanese without incurring enormous losses through futile frontal attacks. Other generals convinced him that a much wiser plan would be "to surround the area and cut off all supplies, accompanied by plenty of mortar fire and constant harassing." It would take longer, but such a strategy would kill and wound far fewer American and Australian soldiers.

"This seemed to me very slow work," Eichelberger told Gen. Edmund F. Herring, "but I realize that any other decision may result in tremendous loss of personnel without commensurate gains." It had taken Eichelberger a long time to realize what General Harding had known in the first place—and what the Supreme Commander of the Southwest Pacific forces either didn't know or didn't want to know.

Surround-and-harass became the new task of the weary Americans. Crack Aussie troops were given the job of winding up the Buna campaign by taking Sanananda.

Outnumbered two to one by the Japanese defenders, the Aussies attacked enemy forts with tommy guns, grenades, and bayonets. Since the enemy depended largely on swamp country to protect them on the west, they had concentrated their defenses on the dry ground in the east. While General Grose's 127th Infantry kept the Japanese busy, the Aussies plunged through the "impassable" swamp from the west and took the enemy by surprise.

Fierce hand-to-hand fighting ensued. One Aussie brigade fought day and night for five weeks, although they were outnumbered ten to one. Some forts held as many as seventy-five Japanese apiece. It was a valiant fight, but a costly one. The brigade lost 96 percent of its men. But the Japanese 18th Army suffered 16,000 casualties of its own at the hands of the Australian 7th Division.

Unable to hold Sanananda any longer, the enemy withdrew, pursued by Aussie bayonets. Thirty-three more Japanese were killed; the rest escaped north in barges. Humiliated by defeat, Maj. Gen. Kensaku Oda shot himself.

"The Australians are magnificent troops," declared MacArthur happily, "unsurpassed in the world." A U.S. War Department brochure concurred: "They're tough guys. They've been in all the hot spots—wherever the going has been tough. They have the reputation for staying in there and pitching with anything they can get their hands on. And if there isn't anything else, they use their hands. There's no finer soldier in the world!"

By January 23, 1943, the Buna campaign was over, with Buna, Gona, and Sanananda in Allied hands. The 16,000 casualties suffered by the Japanese in the nine-week battle had cost the Aussies almost 5,700 killed, wounded, or missing. On the American side there had been 2,855 casualties out of 11,000 members of the 32nd. But an additional 5,358 were sick with malaria, and the rest were running high fevers. More than 200 Allied soldiers died of scrub typhus.

Following the victory, many Allied soldiers dropped into beach foxholes and slumped into exhausted sleep, their scarecrow limbs akimbo.

Commenting on the ordeal of the 32nd, official U.S. Army historian Samuel Milner related, "There were almost no replacements, and the strength of the units fell steadily until, in a few instances, they were near the extinction point when relieved."

One year later, more than two thousand veterans of the Battle of Buna had to be dropped out of the 32nd's ranks because they were still much too ill to return to combat.

On January 9, 1943, Eichelberger won his decoration, as promised, from MacArthur. The commander-in-chief prayed. "To Almighty God I give thanks for that guidance which has brought us this success in our great crusade. His is the honor, the power and the glory forever. Amen."

Three weeks after the fall of Buna, MacArthur issued a communiqué for "home consumption." He announced that our losses—killed, wounded, and sick—had been low. His explanation of this remarkable "accomplishment" was that there had been no need to hurry and attack, because "the time element was in this case of little importance."

He was contradicted by no less an authority than his immediate subordinate, General Eichelberger himself.

"The statement that 'losses were small because there was no hurry' was one of the great surprises of my life," Eichelberger declared bluntly. "As you know, our Allied losses were heavy, and as commander in the field, I had been told many times of the necessity for speed."

After the costly Battle of Buna ended, it was learned that had MacArthur's intelligence staff been functioning properly, he would have known that the enemy troops in the area lacked sufficient small arms, food, and medical supplies and was suffering great sickness, exhaustion, and hunger. Many Japanese, their feet "red-raw and white-swollen," were hobbling about weakly in bandages instead of boots.

Sgt. Kyoshi Wada wrote in his diary, "We are reduced to eating grass. We are just like horses." By January 10 all the grass and roots in his area had been eaten. The men were starving. One captured Japanese soldier revealed, "We had no medicine for malaria, no food for the

123

company for a week. Finally, we collected the bodies of enemy dead and became cannibals. . . . The patients in our field hospital became living statues, horribly emaciated for lack of food."

When Maj. Mitsuo Koiwai, commanding the 2nd Battalion, 41st Japanese Infantry, was captured, he revealed, "We were in such a position at Buna that we wondered whether the Americans would bypass us and leave us to starve."

Samuel Milner declared bluntly, "It was clear that starvation had been a potent factor in the final reduction of the beachhead and that, had the Allies not been so determined to reduce it by direct attack, hunger would in due course have accomplished the same thing."

Thus MacArthur's decision to swiftly take Buna at all costs had resulted in 8,555 unnecessary American and Australian casualties, unnecessary because if the Japanese in the Buna salient had been left to starve, the base would have fallen into Allied hands without the loss of a single Allied soldier.

MacArthur had justified his orders to Eichelberger to take Buna regardless of the cost in lives because of the necessity for a speedy victory in this area. Yet, when it was all over, MacArthur had blandly issued a communiqué that "losses were small because there was no hurry."

The angry public outcry at his false claim later made MacArthur highly sensitive to the need to issue more believable battle reports.

Aussie war correspondent Johnson called the battle for New Guinea "the toughest fighting in the world." American historian Samuel Eliot Morison described it as "certainly the nastiest of the war."

MacArthur learned a valuable lesson from his tragic mistake. He determined never again to order "a head-on collision of the bloody, grinding type." After Buna he devised a whole new military strategy designed to save Allied lives and at the same time speed up the timetable of victory.

His new tactics called for "leapfrogging" each strong Japanese base, attacking and seizing instead a lightly defended enemy island north of it. He would then rush the construction of airstrips to pound the supply lines of the bypassed troops, leaving them to "wither on the vine," as he should have done at Buna.

Using this technique, he soon immobilized sixty-thousand of the enemy at Hansa Bay, Wewak, and Madang in northern New Guinea, frustrating and bewildering the Japanese commanders there, who had expected direct attacks similar to the Buna campaign.

Much of the fighting the Aussies did in New Guinea was along high, perilous cliffs, where falling was as great a threat to their lives as getting shot.

After the campaign at Buna, the Japanese blocked the way to the vital port of Finschhafen, which they used as a supply base. Atop a sheer cliff called Kakakog Ridge, several companies of their marines manned machine guns in solidly sandbagged positions.

Aussies of the 15th Battalion hacked their way up the cliff with tomahawks, machetes, and bayonets. Sometimes they moved along on hands and knees, sometimes hand over hand along protruding vines and branches. They often hung on by one hand and fired Owen guns or hurled grenades with the other. The Aussies fought their way to the crest under continuous fire. Capturing the thirteen gun positions, they killed half the enemy marines. The others fled in panic.

Later Aussies of the 16th Battalion attacked a force of eight hundred Japanese who had complete command of a strategic 5,700-foot sheer peak known as the Pimple, which soared above Shaggy Ridge. Machine-gun pits en-

American GIs pour out of an LST on the beach at Saidor. (U. S. National Archives)

circled the peak. The ridge was so narrow that two men could not pass each other.

The Aussies ascended the Pimple in single file, fighting the Japanese hand to hand, from dugout to dugout. They blew up enemy bunkers by tossing in canisters of high explosives attached to grenades. Some of the enemy committed suicide by leaping off the ridge. The Aussies won the Battle of Shaggy Ridge at a cost of 46 killed, 147 wounded. But the Japanese lost at least 500 marines along with the strategic eyrie.

Aussie troops dig in on a newly captured height on Shaggy Ridge. (Australian War Memorial)

In another ridge battle, one Aussie company of the 58th Battalion was ordered to withdraw because the Japanese defenses seemed impregnable. Sgt. Tom Derrick begged for one last chance to tackle the job by himself.

Hurling grenade after grenade, he wiped out no less than ten enemy posts, one after another. He would dash forward and hurl his grenades from a range of only six yards. What a whole company couldn't do in the face of withering machine-gun fire, one tough Aussie from Adelaide did single-handed.

He was awarded the Victoria Cross.

10
Praise the Lord and Pass the Spinach

In my sector of New Guinea, things quieted down when the fighting switched from Milne Bay to the Buna front. The bombing continued regularly, sometimes during the day but mostly at night.

Mail finally arrived by freighter for the first time in three months. At a nighttime mail call we gathered eagerly for the letters we had been awaiting. I received eleven letters from my wife.

Unable to wait until I was back in my tent to read them, I ripped one open and began reading it by flashlight as I made my way back to my tent. I fell into a trench, pulled myself out, and continued to read as I walked. A few moments later I stumbled over a bucket of water. But no number of accidents could have stopped me from reading on eagerly.

By this time I had been authorized as a war correspondent, in addition to my military duties, by MacArthur's order. For *Look* magazine I did a picture story of our jungle hospital. This mobile treatment center, set up by the Medical Corps, was one of the first in duty overseas. Here precious moments were saved, allowing surgeons to operate within an hour after a soldier was wounded.

The jungle hospital had up to five hundred cots and was equipped to give medical care for a month or longer. A laboratory did blood counts, analyses for malaria and tropical fever, and other tests. The nurses were all men— tough GIs, but incredibly gentle with patients.

I followed the treatment of a wounded twenty-four-year-old Air Corps waist-gunner from Taylor, Washington, Sgt. William Charles Simon. He had been hit while flying a mission in a Liberator, one of the B-24s of the group known as the Jolly Rogers, against an enemy cruiser. His bomber had been attacked by ten Zeros. Simon had shot down two before being hit in the arm, waist, and groin. As his B-24 fled back to its base, Simon's leg felt numb. He couldn't move the fingers of his left hand, and his breathing came hard.

Simon collapsed as the plane touched down. He was taken off and rushed to the field hospital. The ambulance driver tried to make the swift ride over the terrible road as smooth as possible.

Simon's wounds were promptly X-rayed. In five minutes bullets were found in a rib, and shell scraps in his forearm and groin. He was treated for shock and quickly operated on by two doctors under a long pyramidal tent. Afterward an internist checked Simon's heart and lungs to see if the bullets had done any further damage. Then

Medical Corps Captain Leonard Stalker with a native whose broken arm he fixed.

Medical officers at the jungle hospital. Captain Leonard Stalker is second from left.

Medics carry a convalescing GI over a medics-built bridge to the river for a bath.

he was carried to the river on a stretcher to be bathed. A soldier sat on the bank with a rifle as a lookout for crocodiles.

When his dressings needed changing, Simon was taken to a special tent where instruments were kept as sterile as possible. The doctors here dressed over a thousand wounds in a typical month. Soon Simon was well enough to hobble around on crutches, and then to discard them. Air raids frequently sent him, with hospital corpsmen and other patients, to slit trenches. Surgeons, however, often continued operating even while enemy bombers were blasting the area.

I was on hand to shake Bill Simon's hand as, fully recovered from his wounds, he left the jungle hospital to

Medics carry wounded waist gunner Sgt. William Charles Simon into the operating tent at the jungle hospital.

Jungle hospital, New Guinea.

return to the Jolly Rogers. Coincidentally, the following year, I transferred into the Jolly Rogers myself, and I tried to look him up. I learned that after completing the required fifty combat missions and being scheduled to return to the States, he had agreed to his pilot's offhand suggestion that the crew go on "just one last mission." On that flight their B-24 had been shot down, and all aboard were lost.

In my capacity as war correspondent I did a lot of flying with various Air Corps units at Milne Bay. I continued this practice during a second hitch in New Guinea the following year.

On January 17, 1943, the Japanese struck Milne Bay with a flight of twenty-three bombers flying wingtip to wingtip, stretching across the entire base. A squadron of Zeros accompanied them as top cover. The bombers dropped daisy-cutters that sent shrapnel flying horizontally all around us at knee level. The Red Alert, fortunately, had sent most of us jumping into our slit trenches.

Convalescing Sgt. William Charles Simon buys a grass skirt from natives at the jungle hospital.

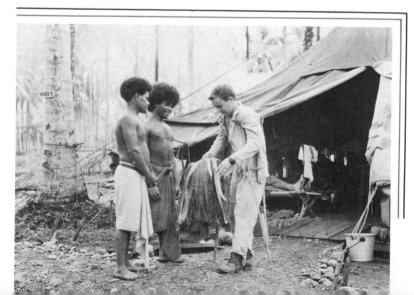

Sgt. William Charles Simon, wounded Jolly Rogers waist gunner, who was killed flying one last mission he didn't have to fly.

GI war correspondent Archer in front of a war strategy map of New Guinea in Milne Bay.

The raid smashed nine of our bombers and a P-39 fighter. Three oil trucks and eight fuel dumps also went up in flames. The bomber airstrip was torn up, huge holes rendering it unusable. That night there were two more Red Alerts, with some spasmodic bombing. In the next twenty-four hours we were hit by four more air raids. Rumors flew that these strikes were softening us up for a new invasion of Milne Bay.

On the next day a new squadron of P-39 fighters flew in to the base to help fight off the enemy bombers. That night the Japanese sent their bombers one at a time, all night long. There was little sleep for us, between the constant bombings and the thud of ack-ack fire vainly probing for the enemy in the dark sky. Some GIs spent the night in slit trenches. I was among those who gave up and took their chances on their cots. The war hadn't killed me thus far, and I counted on my luck to hold out.

After a few nights had passed without raids, the base decided to help morale by screening a war film called "Next of Kin" in a clearing. A Red Alert siren sent watching GIs diving for shelter, until they realized that the siren had emanated from the movie. Returning sheepishly, they sat through a second siren. There were four terrific explosions nearby a few minutes later. This time it had been the real thing.

The area was cleared in ten seconds. The following night the projectionist tried to screen the film again, but he gave up after persistent Red Alerts. We never did find out how "Next of Kin" ended.

On my second night on duty at the Fighter Sector, bombs began falling close to our tent. I joined the controller and all the men on shift in diving under the plotting table. One of my men caught shrapnel just above his ear, but fortunately he was wearing his helmet.

After the tenth enemy raid in three days, we were groggy from lack of sleep. The antiaircraft batteries expended 942 rounds of ammunition on one raid alone.

When intensive daylight raids pinned us in the trenches, we passed the dreary time playing cards until the All Clear sounded.

Japanese radio commentators from Rabaul kept threatening us with a new invasion if we didn't get out of Milne Bay. Many GIs were edgy. At the sound of a rifle shot, some men would rush for their weapons, convinced enemy marines had landed again.

Our unit organized a twenty-four-mile march through the battleground as a training precaution. The jungle was alive with the shrill cries of tropical birds as we pressed through thick tangles of vegetation and waded through streams. We had to hold handkerchiefs to our noses when we passed still-unburied Japanese corpses.

The area was a chaos of shell holes, blasted trees, smashed invasion barges. We passed the KB Mission, which had been reduced to ruins in the fierce fighting that had raged around it. We returned to base with a fresh appreciation of the prowess of the Aussie infantry in challenging and defeating the enemy in that steaming tropical hell.

As a correspondent I was able to talk to some captured Japanese officers who knew a few words of English. "No like Tojo [Japan's war minister]," one assured me, shaking his head. He waved his hand. "No like rat-a-tat-tat." He mimicked using a tommy gun. Then he clasped one hand with the other. "Britain, Japan, United States—like that!" I asked how he was being treated. "Happy," he beamed. "Thank you very much!"

Another prisoner answered my questions defiantly through an interpreter. "Japan will never surrender!" he snapped. "You may take Lae, but you will never recapture Moresby! We will win because our troops are already in Townsville and California!"

Many Japanese troops were deceived by Tokyo as to the true military situation.

During our last few weeks in Milne Bay a severe fungus infection known as "jungle rot" put me in the hospital for a week. Finally, orders came for our relief, and on February 22, 1943, we boarded a Dutch East Indies freighter, the S.S. *Kom Der Lijn*, for a rest period in Townsville.

As we left port the air raid siren wailed. We felt naked with no slit trench to run to. But the bombs were aimed at the airfield, and our old tub of a ship lumbered hastily out into the China Straits. Now all we had to do was reach Australia before some enemy submarine could target us.

The journey took two days. We had departed so hastily that there were insufficient provisions on board. Hungry GIs openly booed the officers, who were fed three

Townsville, Australia. The author teaches jujitsu to his company.

good meals a day. The officers took to staying out of sight.

When we disembarked at Mareeba in a rainstorm, we were loaded aboard a train for Townsville. The war was over for us for a brief while. We felt safe.

I was reunited with my wife in Townsville. We took an apartment off the post. During one weekend off duty when we took a trip to Magnetic Island, we had the unusual experience of watching a battle between a whale and a shark about a mile offshore.

I now came down with malaria and had to be hospitalized. I also broke my ankle while teaching jujitsu to the men in camp. But these were small prices for the

Two Yanks with Australian brides talk it over. Author is on the left.

An Australian pub. (Australian Department of Information)

pleasure of spending five months in Australia. During this time we were issued new equipment for improved Fighter Sector operations and were trained in its use.

On August 10 we headed back to the jungle island on a freighter whose decks were loaded with incendiary bombs piled next to barrels of gas and highly inflammable varnishes. Enemy submarines still prowled the Coral Sea, and enemy bombers still blasted our attempts to reinforce New Guinea. But what bothered us most, once again, was the food situation.

We were on board five days, living on only two almost inedible meals a day. Some GIs broke into the hold and hijacked dozens of loaves of bread. Surplus loaves sold for $6.50 each.

I sought out a first lieutenant I shall call Baxter, who was now in command of our plotting platoon. The radar platoons had left separately for New Guinea outposts. Our platoon had been attached to a fighter control squadron headed for the Markham Valley, where the Aussies were fighting.

A small man, Baxter seemingly suffered from a chronic sense of inferiority. As a civilian he had worked on road-building crews and had gained his commission through the National Guard. We had been on friendly terms during our first hitch in New Guinea, when he had been a second lieutenant with little authority. He had even shared my exasperation at the often stupid preoccupation of superior officers with petty Army regulations, at the expense of unit morale and performance of our duty.

I asked him now to talk to the transport commmander about getting us some decent food and a third meal, even if it was only bread and coffee. He refused, shrugging off the men's hunger. I stared at him in surprise. This was my first intimation that Baxter would not go to bat for his men when they had a just grievance. It was not to be the last.

When we reached Port Moresby, native rafts towed us ashore. We were handed new pills to ward off malaria. Trucks took us to a staging area; our barracks bags were supposed to follow separately. When they finally arrived, six of the bags had been slit open and looted.

I asked Baxter to report the thefts to the MPs. He refused, stating that he was not going to have us called "a bunch of crybabies."

Our next clash came within a matter of hours. In the staging area he ordered me to have our men pitch pup tents and sleep on the ground. I couldn't believe my ears. The staging area at Port Moresby now had hundreds of tents, with cots set up. At least half the tents were empty. Most of our men, in fact, had already moved into them.

141

American troops disembarking at Port Moresby. (U.S. National Archives)

When I protested, he replied that the order came from staging area officers, and that was that. I pointed out that it was obvious they were ignoring us because we were an attached platoon without a high-ranking officer. He angrily accused me of "babying" the men and reminded me that I was supposed to be the third officer of the platoon—"not the men's union representative!"

When I transmitted his order to clear out of the large tents and to pitch pup tents instead, there was an outraged roar of protest. The five-day crossing of the Coral Sea had been hot and brutal, and most of the men slept poorly, sprawled on the hot deck every night. With empty tents and cots available now, they saw no reason to sleep on the ground.

It occurred to me that Baxter's failure to look after the welfare of our men was related to his obsequious, almost cringing, behavior toward officers of higher rank. Was he afraid that he would antagonize them and perhaps hurt his chances for promotion if he spoke up for our men?

His conduct would not have been unusual in a stateside training camp. But we were now veterans of half a year's fighting. The men were no longer green recruits. And in the combat zone, officers and men worked together as a team. You didn't go by the book in the frontline areas of New Guinea. Since we were headed back into action, I felt strongly that Baxter should have strengthened platoon morale by pressing the men's cause.

After four nights of sleeping on the ground, Baxter came into camp from officers' quarters at 10:00 P.M. and ordered me to wake everybody. We were slated to fly out over the Owen Stanley Range in C-47 transports, along with forty-three tons of our bulky new equipment, which took nineteen 2½-ton trucks to move.

We wrestled this backbreaking tonnage onto the trucks by the light of their headlights. As the evening stars faded over the palms, we threw our barracks bags into the trucks and jumped on. Near dawn our convoy sped out to the airstrip.

The sun was blazing by the time each truck had found its assigned transport and backed up to it. We began the job of loading the C-47s with our one-ton generators, jeeps, trailers, five-hundred-pound gas drums, and heavy electrical equipment, using no loading equipment except one-foot-wide metal ramps. As we squeezed, lifted, and shoved those forty-three tons into the planes, the C-47s' metal bodies heated up diabolically in the tropic sun.

Loading the jeeps was hardest of all. First a jeep had to be driven carefully up two narrow ramps aligned with the wheels, until it was partway through the plane door, which had not been designed as a garage entrance. Then four of us had to grab what grips we could and bump the jeep up and down to slide it over an inch at a time, allowing the driver to nose it inside the plane a little further. This had to be repeated until the jeep was far enough inside to turn and drive up the slanted floor to the front. One slight miscalculation and the jeep's rear wheels would have slid off the narrow ramps.

When we rolled the gas drums up the ramps and along the floor of the plane, we warily eyed the sparks flying beneath our feet.

At last enough equipment was loaded on each plane to make up the allotted maximum freightage, and everything was lashed securely with ropes. To lash down a jeep, three of us had to jump on the bumper until there was no rope slack that might let the jeep become a loose cannon in the bumpy air pockets that abounded over the Owen Stanley Range.

At noon we were still groaning under the weight of the equipment we were muscling, by which time the C-47s seemed two degrees away from bursting into flame and roasting us alive.

144

As a master sergeant, I was not required to work side by side with the men. But I chose to share their ordeal because I knew of no other way to deserve their respect. I genuinely believed in democracy, army or no army.

At last everything was loaded and secured. We collapsed under the bountiful shade of the transports' wings.

Lieutenant Baxter showed up at the airstrip in a jeep. He was clean-shaven and neatly uniformed, and he had none of the dark circles under his eyes that were under ours.

"Unload the planes," he told me with a bland little smile. "We're not going today. Get all the equipment back on the trucks. And when you get back to the staging area, unload it off the trucks."

I stared at him, speechless. He drove off.

Our ordeal was repeated like a film run backward. Everything was dragged, pulled, and lifted out of the planes and onto the trucks. By this time all of us were half naked, our torsos glistening with rivers of sweat. Our truck convoy wound wearily back to camp. Parched and exhausted, we then had to wrestle all the equipment off the nineteen trucks before we could collapse into our pup tents.

Incredibly, this fiasco was repeated *three times*.

On our third endeavor, I urged Baxter to speak to the proper authorities for permission to let our forty-three tons of equipment stay loaded on the transports, while we slept under the planes' wings until the weather over the Owen Stanleys permitted us to fly out. He refused, then drove back to the officers' club in his spotless uniform.

On the fourth day we once more loaded the C-47s in numb despair. We could scarcely believe it when, this time, the weather over the Owen Stanleys was reported favorable and the word was go. We boarded the flying freight cars, and collapsed around the cargo, too weary to stare out at the corrugated mountain range which began sliding past beneath us.

By this time each man in the platoon had personally lifted eight tons as his share in the move. We had worked at high noon, when the transports were blistering furnaces. The backbreaking loading and unloading, on two meals a day with only one canteen of water, had sent one man to the field hospital with a crushed foot, another with a kidney-stone attack.

P-38s and P-39s accompanied us overhead to protect us from Zeros. As we flew over the Owen Stanleys, the tall kunai grass below reached up toward us like the jagged pikes of a palace gate. Mountain slopes rose beneath us, the nearest green, the farthest an autumn tan. The slopes ran into one another like clasped fingers. Where they joined, small forests nestled. From great heights the Markham River Valley, deprived of rain, resembled anatomical charts of the nervous system. It was hard to distinguish rivers from riverbeds, except where telltale flashes mirrored the sunlight.

Shortly before dark the cargo planes touched down in a partially sunlit valley. This was Nadzab, in the Markham Valley. The grass airstrip had just been seized from the enemy. A smashed transport was tilted on its side at the edge of the strip. Fighting was still going on throughout the valley.

Because enemy planes bombed the airstrip several times a day to prevent our troops and supplies from being flown in, the C-47s had to be unloaded at lightning speed. The doors flew open, and the exhausted GIs staggered around trying once more to hastily unload the forty-three tons of equipment. They disembarked three jeeps and two trailers at a furious pace, then dragged off the rest of the heavy cargo and lifted it on to the vehicles. The cargo doors slammed, and the C-47s zoomed off.

We had made it. But more ordeals were in store for us.

11
Rebellion in the Jungle

"Sergeant," Lieutenant Baxter said, "take the jeeps and trailers down into that gully next to the river. We'll have good natural camouflage there."

The gully, cloaked by trees, was almost thirty feet lower than the valley floor. I stared down dubiously. The New Guinea rainy season was about due. I pointed out that torrential rains would raise the river, flooding the gully.

"Once we take those forty-three tons down there and the rain turns everything to mud," I warned Baxter, "we'll never be able to get the equipment out." The other noncoms raced up to make the same protest. Baxter stared at us in vexation.

"You're *always* arguing with me!" he snapped. "Just remember who's in command here! We've got to get under cover fast before we're raided. Get that stuff into the gully, pronto!"

We did. Our jeep convoy descended precipitously toward a shallow stream, where we pitched camp. I supervised the setting up of a Fighter Sector tent. We moved our new equipment in and began operations over a large map table of the area we had prepared. Men who could be spared strung jungle hammocks between trees and fell into an exhausted slumber.

Within forty-eight hours a squadron of American-flown P-47 fighters was stationed at the airstrip, along with a few Aussie antiaircraft batteries. The base was quickly operational, despite some enemy air raids.

On our ninth day the rainy season set in. The river began to rise ominously. Then it burst its banks and rolled through the gully. The water rose around our feet in the Fighter Sector tent as we were plotting the course of enemy bombers flying toward us. I ordered the men to stay at their posts as long as possible to continue taking phone and radio reports from our radar stations and spotters.

The controller waded out to high ground and ran to his headquarters to set up an emergency Fighter Sector for a transfer of operations. Meanwhile, the flood grew hip-high and was still rising. Water snakes, giant centipedes, and other tropical river creatures writhed through the fast-flowing waters around us. One man stood guard on top of the plotting table, rifle in hand, watching for the crocodiles that frequently swam in the flooded lowlands during the *guba* season. The rest of the men on shift with me continued tracking the enemy bombers.

When the flood reached table level, I looked around for

Lieutenant Baxter. He was, not surprisingly, absent. I finally gave orders to my men to leave their posts and swim for it. I remained with the flooded setup, keeping all lines open, and shouted up information on the enemy flight to Air Corps officers in the valley. They transmitted the information to the emergency Fighter Sector.

Finally the controller notified me that our fighter planes were airborne and had intercepted the enemy planes. Free to leave, I dove into the swirling floodwaters and swam to safety.

When I located Baxter, his face was drawn and white. He avoided my eyes, and he did not speak to any of the men. I knew he was secretly dreading any leak to the Fighter Control Squadron officers that he had stubbornly insisted on moving our operations into the gully, despite the specific warnings we noncoms had given him about flooding.

We lost all our expensive equipment. Duplicate equipment had to be flown in to us from Australia. We set up new operations in a camouflaged pyramidal tent at the edge of the valley floor.

The controller in charge of the Fighter Sector was always a pilot with the rank of captain, major, or colonel. Because seconds counted once enemy flights had been reported, he and the ack-ack officer needed to confer frequently with our platoon officer in charge of plotting operations.

Our filter officer was supposed to do this, but in practice I did it during my twelve-hour shifts, and I assigned one of my sergeants when I was off duty. The filter officer, whom I'll call Second Lieutenant Spoorie, had been a supply officer, and he was both uninterested in and unqualified for the job. He preferred to stay in his tent and leave the work to me. That was all right with me, because a lot of lives at the base were at stake, and my men and I knew what we were doing.

Incensed, Baxter put himself on duty in the Fighter

Sector. But to his chagrin he found that, despite the airs of command he assumed by giving unnecessary orders to the men on shift, during raids the controller and ack-ack officer bypassed him to work with me, or one of my sergeants if I was off shift.

Baxter threw a fit and raged at me privately that the controller was supposed to ask him, not me, for information. I suggested that he complain to the colonel, not to me, and asked if he wanted me to refuse to answer the colonel's questions. He stalked off in fury.

I was the one who had taught Baxter the little he understood about Fighter Sector operations. I had also helped him exchange his gold bar for a silver one by writing a new Standard Operating Procedure for Fighter Sector operations in the forward area. This had been submitted to battalion headquarters over his signature. I didn't mind letting him take credit, as long as he didn't interfere with our operational efficiency.

Baxter's incompetence sometimes had humorous overtones. One time he watched me, at the controller's request, predict the course of flight of an enemy plane whose track our radar had lost after a position placing it 250 miles north of us. I made my calculations and projected a flight that took the enemy to a certain coordinate by 11:09 A.M. At exactly 11:06 a different radar picked up the "bogey" where I had predicted.

The next day I was handling another enemy track when, to my surprise, Baxter motioned me to stand aside and took over. The radar lost the track about fifty miles from our base. To my amazement Baxter continued to project the bogey's course on the grid with wooden arrows, saying nothing to the controller.

The controller called a Red Alert and scrambled a flight of fighters to intercept. Ack-Ack alerted its batteries and gave the grid coordinates of Baxter's projected flight. The pilots in the air soon reported in puzzlement that they could see nothing of the bogey. The controller stared at the arrows, which indicated the position of the enemy as being almost directly overhead.

"Where'd those reports come from?" he asked Baxter.

Baxter blinked. "Why, it's a projection. It's where I figured the bogey would be by now if he stayed on course."

The disgusted controller ordered the scrambled flight back to base and called off the Red Alert. Then in a weary voice he explained to Baxter that no projected flight ever appeared on the table unless the controller ordered it and knew about it.

That didn't stop Baxter's desperate bid for prestige. He saw a chance to throw his weight around when he got his hands on a copy of a new Standard Operating Procedure sent up from Australia by battalion headquarters. I had found that it was impossible to follow this SOP without fouling up our whole operation, which was not yet geared for all the changes.

I told my men to use their best judgment. But Baxter stormed at me that I must follow the new SOP to the letter.

I did so. Within one day the Fighter Sector was thrown into confusion and uproar. The controller was in a murderous rage because all the flight reports were fouled up. When he asked me what the devil I thought I was doing, I explained that I was following Lieutenant Baxter's orders. After ten sulphurous minutes of being chewed out savagely by the colonel, a red-faced Baxter ordered me to forget the new SOP and use my best judgment.

The enemy air command was wily enough without blunders in our Fighter Sector making it easier for them to bomb our base. One day I happened to be watching a group of our B-25s from Port Moresby flying diagonally across our airstrip on a mission north of us. Two minutes later another flight of bombers at the same altitude flew behind the first from a different direction, but then swerved to make runs directly over the airstrip.

I saw the red balls on the fuselages at the same time that a wind indicator spiraled down from the lead plane. Then the bombs fell, churning up the airstrip in huge clouds of dust.

A second flight of B-25s came behind, apparently part of the echelon of the first flight. The Japanese had shrewdly skipped over the mountain range to position themselves between two B-25 formations, confusing everybody—the Fighter Sector, the ack-ack batteries, and our planes in the sky—until the bombs fell. After that they swerved back over the mountain and disappeared.

One day it was quiet in the Fighter Sector. Our plotters were reading at their posts around the map table. The controller, a flying lieutenant colonel, sat on the elevated wooden bench polishing off reports of the day's activities.

A plotter's phone rang. All books and papers were instantly pushed aside. The plotter pinned the headset to his ear, listened intently, and wrote furiously in his log. Reading over his shoulder, I placed a colored wooden arrow at the reported coordinates on the map table, representing a flight 150 miles northeast, heading toward our base.

"Target!" I called out. "Four unidentified bombers, very high, heading southwest at ten thousand feet. Time of origin—one eight five three." The plotter set up an information tree next to the arrow on the table.

"Red Alert!" the controller ordered. He pressed a button that lit a red electric bulb over the plotting table. Then he picked up his phone to scramble our fighter planes.

Our base at Nadzab in the Markham Valley is hit by Japanese bombers.

One of our men at a switchboard flashed the word to all units at the base as the sirens moaned. An Aussie antiaircraft officer rang his headquarters to report the position and direction of the enemy flight. Ack-ack gunners all over the base leaped into their pits, ready for action.

As further reports on the enemy flight came in from Aussie coast-watchers hidden in enemy territory, I placed new arrows on the table map and called out the new information. This data was swiftly relayed to the ack-ack batteries and to the fighter planes now roaring up to intercept the enemy.

We could hear the thunder of bomber engines approaching, the sound waves rolling across the open valley. The colonel in charge of the fighter squadron burst into the Fighter Sector to listen to the air-to-ground conversation between the controller and the fighter pilots attacking the bombers.

"Fuel low. Coming in. Get out of the way!"

"Roger. Do you see Baker Two?"

"Saw him go into the drink."

"Any coral islands near him?

"No. Can anyone help?"

"Will try. Come in—field clear."

The sky was filled with bursting flak as the Aussie ack-ack gunners sought the range of the bombers. Enemy motors whined loudly overhead, like angry hawks.

Another voice came tensely over the air-ground. "I'm going down. Going down. Wounded. No controls . . ."

"Bail out!" cried the controller. "For God's sake, bail out!"

An eerie whistling, followed by a diving, screeching sound that grew to a roar, sent all of us diving to the ground. A second later, ear-shattering explosions blasted frighteningly close to our tent.

"Four," counted the fighter squadron commander from a prone position, looking at his watch. "Hundred-pounders, most likely."

"Wow," one of my men sighed. "I thought they were landing in my hip pocket."

"Don't worry," a second plotter assured him, lifting his face above the plotting table. "They weren't aiming at us."

"I'd feel safer if they were!"

After the raid one of my sergeants asked me why we had to stay at the plotting table once the Japanese were right over us and our fighters and the ack-ack had visual contact; we couldn't do anything more after that.

I talked to the controller about letting my men run for slit trenches at those times, and he agreed. But when I broached the subject with Baxter, he refused. So we continued to be standing targets during the day-and-night strafing and bombing attacks that pounded Nadzab. We never saw Baxter during these raids, except for one night when a Red Alert turned into a raid while he was still in the Fighter Sector.

As enemy planes droned overhead, daisy-cutters began screaming down from the sky. A string of them came toward us with increasing volume. The noise was deafening and frightening.

Then, violent explosions.

I looked around and saw Baxter crawling underneath the plotting table. Our eyes met for a moment. He flushed and looked away. My men stood quietly, contemptuously, at their posts around the table. After the raid Baxter had nothing to say to us. Pale and shaking, he left the operations tent immediately.

Dengue, malaria, jungle rot, and blackwater fever kept us constantly shorthanded. We often had to work sixteen-hour shifts. Several of the men came to me asking that they be permitted to volunteer for a permanent night shift. This was satisfactory to the whole platoon, and it would also have solved the scheduling headaches that illness caused. Baxter refused to hear of it.

12

"Lieutenant, Sir, You're Crazy!"

Platoon morale kept going from bad to worse, as Baxter lost no opportunity to antagonize the men. He saw the conflict as a struggle between them and himself. He grew more and more repressive in the effort to assert his authority.

Most of my men did the best job they could at their post in spite of him. They knew its importance to the safety of troops and planes at the base. If they hated Baxter, they respected the Air Corps officers working with us.

I explained the situation to the commanding officer of the squadron to which we were attached, and pointed out that morale was also low because none of our men had been given promotions after two years of overseas duty. He was disturbed enough about it to promise that he would see what could be done about promotions for our men, even if Baxter wouldn't.

Bad blood between Baxter and the men came to a boil when he called a special meeting of noncoms. He accused us of being inefficient and of "babying" the men. One sergeant pointed out resentfully that our outfit had won a special commendation from Fifth Air Force headquarters.

"So what?" Baxter rasped. From now on, he said, there was going to be a completely new regimen. Instead of being granted time off to rest and look after themselves, all men would be compelled to attend classes in military courtesy, do close-order drill, and stand daily reveille, retreat, and inspections. This was in addition to working regular shifts at the Fighter Sector or on camp details and sweating out constant air raids.

The trouble with us noncoms, Baxter insisted, was that we wouldn't push the men. *That* was why morale was so low.

A stunned silence followed his remarks. None of us could believe our ears. This was the New Guinea combat zone. We were combat veterans. We were still being hit with one or two enemy raids daily. We never got enough rest in the murderous heat. And now Baxter wanted to add on a program of what GIs contemptuously called "stateside chicken"—petty rules and regulations to keep recruits busy and dominated. In the *jungle?*

I warned him that he could have a mutiny on his hands.

Every noncom in the outfit put his stripes on the line by refusing to carry out his orders, challenging Baxter to demote them all to the rank of private. Purple with rage, he shrieked that no one would be allowed to resign his rank.

I asked for clarification of his orders. Was he ordering me to attend all these formations and classes with the platoon? At first he yelled that I was to attend, but he suddenly changed his mind when I reminded him that obviously I couldn't continue to spend twelve hours a day on duty at the Fighter Sector if I was attending every class and formation.

Our first reveille formation in the jungle the next morning was the real beginning of the mutiny. Baxter was there in the cold dawn, to show the men that he was going to "soldier" too. A third of the men refused to fall out from their tents.

What followed was one of the most disgraceful scenes I had ever witnessed in the Army. The men in formation commented loudly and profanely on what they thought of Baxter and his orders. He turned pale, but made no attempt to discipline anyone. Even when the platoon was called to attention, a voice rang out clearly and defiantly.

"Lieutenant, sir, you're crazy!"

The voice belonged to our cook. Baxter pretended not to have heard. When the formation was dismissed, the whole platoon broke out in derisive catcalls, jeers, and boos. The cook's accusation was repeated by a dozen loud voices. Baxter hurried off to his tent, worried because officers from other outfits had become curious about the uproar and had gathered at our area.

That was only the beginning. It became apparent at every turn that the whole platoon was united in open defiance. When the men were forced to hold a class in military courtesy under some jungle palms, they "gold-bricked" openly. Once they gave cigarettes to some natives to do tribal dances for them.

Baxter saw all this, but he was afraid to back up his orders with any disciplinary action.

I had a hard time trying to keep the platoon in line.

Privates were openly insolent to Baxter, challenging him to do something about it. Although he would grow pale, he would try to pass off such incidents as jokes. He grew afraid of open revolt, or even a bullet in the dark. He began to issue even more exasperating, repressive orders, but always through me. He never dared give the orders himself, for fear the men would merely jeer and tell him to get lost.

Things became so bad that I couldn't get the men to obey any orders they knew came from Baxter. Once seven of my men refused to dig a slit trench near the portion of the river Baxter used as his private swimming hole. Three of them had just come off an eight-hour shift and were due to go back in another eight hours. The sergeant in charge of the shift told me, "Tell Baxter he can throw us all in the guardhouse. We *dare* him!"

I reported their refusal to Baxter and asked him if he wanted me to place them under arrest. I, of course, was on their side, and I was trying to make Baxter understand the stupidity of his behavior in antagonizing the whole platoon.

Baxter glared at me with psychopathic fury. His face was white and drawn, and he looked like an animal in a trap.

"That's what *you* have six stripes for!" he snarled. "It's your job to *make* them follow my orders!"

I told him he could have my stripes back any time he wanted. Why did he expect the men to obey my six stripes when they openly defied his silver bar? If he was going to persist in his crazy orders, I suggested he ought to at least order the arrest of the men who refused to obey. He didn't dare, I knew, because he was afraid that a court-martial would expose the way he'd been mishandling the platoon.

The more Baxter tried to force the platoon to its knees, the more the men fought back. They flooded him with requests for transfers, which he furiously and illegally tore up. When he asked any noncom a question, the noncom would shrug and look dumb: "Why ask me, Lieutenant? I'm just a plain old buck sergeant." Privates began telling him to his face what they thought of him. His only response was to turn on his heel and walk away.

He began spending most of his time in his tent, drinking and brooding. For days on end, his absence allowed the platoon's operations to run smoothly. I began to feel a little sorry for him. Even his fellow officers avoided Baxter. He was definitely going to pieces.

The base celebrated Christmas Eve by shooting off Garand rifles, machine guns, .45s, and bursts of ack-ack. We were interrupted by an enemy air raid.

Sometime after the All Clear sounded, when the base was quiet again, I heard a fusillade of rifle shots in our camp area. I jumped out of my mosquito netting, grabbed my .45, and went outside the tent to investigate. Enemy patrols sometimes infiltrated into Yank and Aussie camps at night, stabbing troops in their sleep. But I saw nothing and went back to my cot.

In the morning one of my sergeants told me that there were twelve bullet holes in Baxter's tent. The shots had been sprayed at about head height. I saw Baxter shaving outside his tent. The razor in his hand was trembling. He knew, I knew, and the whole platoon knew that some of our own men had fired those shots.

I knew then that I had to act. Those bullets may have been meant simply to frighten Baxter. Then again, it was an open secret that in combat conditions sometimes an unpopular officer was shot by one of his own men.

There was certainly no future for anyone in a private war between a psychoneurotic officer and his own platoon. I didn't know how to go about bringing on an investigation, but I decided to press charges against Baxter for incompetence.

The following day I spent about nineteen hours at Fighter Sector. We were raided by the enemy five separate times that night, and I stuck with the shift until about 4:00 A.M. That didn't stop Baxter, five hours later, from ordering me to give men off shift close-order drill. Groggy from lack of sleep, I told him that I couldn't because I had something more important to do.

"Is that so?" he jeered. "And what's that?"

I told him I was going to apply for a transfer on the grounds of his incompetence and inefficiency.

He turned colors. Changing his tone, he tried to talk me out of my intention, first by kidding, then by persuasion, then by angry threats. Remaining adamant, I went to the orderly tent and wrote out my request. I alleged that the platoon's commanding officer had destroyed unit morale to the extent that it was impossible for me to do my job properly.

I went to Baxter's tent and handed the letter to him, reminding him that he couldn't stop it from going through channels.

Reading it, he turned white. What made me think battalion officers would back up a noncom against an officer? If I didn't withdraw the letter, he would send one along with it recommending that I be court-martialed for insubordination. I refused, stating that someone had to protect the men before he drove them crazy—and got himself killed doing it.

In a towering rage he ordered me to my tent, relieving me of all duties until further notice.

Battalion headquarters rushed a captain up to Nadzab to investigate the situation informally. He called a meeting of the whole platoon, with the exception of a skeleton force on duty at the Fighter Sector. Baxter and I were both barred from the meeting.

The captain asked questions of the men and learned the whole story. What he heard convinced him that Bax-

161

ter should be removed from the platoon as quickly as possible. When the captain flew back to battalion headquarters, Baxter was taken along, footlocker and all.

There was wild jubilation throughout the camp.

That was the last the platoon saw of Baxter. We later heard he had been transferred to a radar platoon as a supply officer. The conclusion was obvious. He was no longer considered fit to command.

But until Baxter had been judged a victim of "combat fatigue," my men had suffered under his neurotic despotism for a miserable six months in the Markham Valley.

The new C.O. was instantly popular. He went swimming with the men. He pitched in to help build a recreation hut for the platoon. He demanded and got long-postponed promotions for the privates and PFCs. He had additional men sent up from Australia to bring the platoon to full strength. Jungle classes in military courtesy and close-order drills were cancelled. The new C.O. asked nothing of the men except that they do their assigned jobs well.

The men did their jobs better than well. Before the platoon left New Guinea, it won special citations.

13

At Home in the Jungle

During our hitch in the Markham Valley, when we weren't busy with our duties or fighting our calamitous platoon commander, we tried to make ourselves as comfortable as we could. Yankee ingenuity sought to triumph in a strange Melanesian world where head-hunting and cannibalism were still practiced. On an island once considered fit only for lepers and convicted criminals, where green fungus spread over everything we owned that we didn't air regularly—and even over things we did—signs of civilization began to appear. GIs built jungle versions of tent-homes, roads, outdoor theaters, barber shops, laundries, ice houses, club rooms, repair shops, bars, and swimming pools. GIs were undeterred in their search for some of the comforts of home despite the enemy presence thirty miles north, ninety miles to our rear, and constantly overhead.

For the first few nights in the Markham Valley, we slept in jungle hammocks—coffin-like affairs with zippered mosquito-net sides and rain-cover canvas lids. We used inflated water wings as pillows. The shrewdest of our number dug slit trenches directly under their hammocks. When the siren wailed, all they had to do was unzip the netting and fall cozily into the trenches.

When things settled down sufficiently to permit our home-building projects to begin, we abandoned the hammocks for communal tents. No sooner were the tents up than many men went to work felling trees to make tent frames to firm up the canvas to resemble real walls and roofs.

Most waited cautiously—prudently, as it turned out—until the customary two or three shifts of camp sites had been made. When at last it looked as though we had anchored firmly, the cry of "Timber!" echoed through the jungle.

Before we could put a log frame inside a tent, we had to remove the tent carefully from over our cots, clothes racks, and other possessions. This task was akin to whisking a tablecloth from under place settings without regretting it.

While the tents' contents basked in what we hoped would be temporary sunshine, the GI master builders would bustle around digging stump holes, inserting corner logs, and bridging them with beams. If rainclouds suddenly loomed overhead, the job would get done on the double.

The tent pole was raised some two feet above the ground on a box, and the tent was laid over the wooden framework. The sides were then flapped out and propped with poles. The finished product resembled an oversized beach umbrella with a comfortably high, peaked ceiling. This was home.

Termites were a problem in the jungle, too. When GIs found fresh wood chaff on the floor, they fatalistically awaited the day someone would bring the tent down around their heads by adding the weight of his shirt to a nail on one of the beams.

A greater torment of the New Guinea jungle was the persistent mosquito, which attacked every inch of exposed flesh. GIs who stood guard at night were constantly slapping and scratching at themselves. The anopheles mosquito, which carried malaria, raised its tail when it bit.

The Aussies loved to tell tall tales about the mosquitoes. One Aussie insisted that he had watched one mosquito poke its head through his mosquito netting, while a second mosquito seized its legs and pushed it through.

One morning I woke up to witness one of the strangest sights I had ever seen. A weird variety of huge mosquitoes, which I was told were called Scotch Grays, had formed a living chain, one holding onto the other, in a loop that linked one part of the tent to another. The Scotch Grays, I was told, did not bite humans.

When a "bomber's moon" was bright in the sky for a fortnight, the occupants of one tent found themselves climbing out of their cots and hiking to their trenches three and four times a night. They solved the problem by digging a deep slit trench right in the middle of their tent.

The men learned to make themselves more comfortable by using discarded materials for their home furnishings. One ingenious group mounted their tent pole on a giant wire reel set on end, giving the occupants a modern, double-decker, circular table. Empty food crates, piled sidewise and nailed one on top of the other, provided storage shelves for clothes, toilet articles, and other necessities.

Hinges attached to empty packing cases transformed them into footlockers. As a touch of luxury, some tents had rugs made of sewn flour sacks, useful for keeping mud off shoes and feet.

The interior decoration of most tents was rather stereotyped, consisting in most cases of reminders of the most absent members of the human species—female pinups. Ashtrays were made from the inverted tops of food ration tins. Lengths of old field wire became clotheslines. Empty tins of fruit from home became weatherproof vaults for film and watches. Lamp shades were cut and carved from the sides of tin ration cans.

There was little the Army threw away that GIs couldn't find some use for to make jungle life more bearable.

It was only to be expected that men who could turn rubbish into home furnishings would be adept at repairing things. Our watches were kept in repair by a former farm boy who, back home, had taken watches apart and put them together again for fun. He was so skilled at it that he took one bad wristwatch and one bad pocket watch and created a hybrid that kept perfect time. Within five minutes he could also troubleshoot defects in our cameras, fountain pens, and cigarette lighters. I gained a new respect for Yankee ingenuity.

No self-respecting jungle soldier subsisted solely on meager and tasteless GI mess rations. Preparing private meals in tents was a highly regarded pastime, and fellows with culinary skills were in great demand as tent partners. The supreme chef in our outfit was a little roly-poly Virginia boy whose homemade fudge made him famous throughout camp.

Native fruits provided fine snacks. Pawpaws were purchased from natives at the cost of a used razor blade each, for thirst-quenching refreshment. Natives also supplied very green banana stalks which GIs placed in barracks bags and hung from the tent pole to ripen.

What few amenities we had received in Milne Bay had come from the Australian Salvation Army, not the Red Cross—stationery, magazines, toothpaste, soap, and so on. The Salvation Army also set up units close to the front line and served hot coffee and donuts to weary soldiers. The GIs who served in New Guinea retained a lifelong admiration for the Sallies' dedication to the front-line soldier.

We received almost nothing in the way of PX supplies. When a rare shipment arrived, we usually were allowed only one article per man, in order to make sure there would be enough supplies to go around. The Aussies generously let us buy beer, chocolate, and tobacco at their own PX.

Razor blades were in such short supply that some GIs obtained the necessary permission to grow beards, with the proviso that they wear them for at least three months.

Infantry in New Guinea now had the latest jungle equipment, including a waterproof match box with compass, a flint, and canned heat. In rain, fire could be started by striking a mess-kit knife on the flint so that sparks reached and ignited the canned heat.

Packages of cookies and sweets from home had to be quickly consumed—the ants in New Guinea had little respect for private property. Even biscuits wrapped in cardboard and wax paper weren't safe. Night-raiding field rats hurdled the shelves, tore the containers to bits, and polished off the goodies.

For revenge, one soldier put some sweets on the upper end of a plank balanced above a water barrel. He explained his "better mousetrap" to incredulous tentmates. When the rat ran up the plank for the food, its weight would tip the plank and itself into the barrel and the rat would drown. This bizarre invention earned cries of derision until dawn revealed one large and very drowned rat in the barrel.

A washroom was sometimes a washstand built outdoors against a tree. More often it consisted of a soldier's bucketlike steel helmet. Water was hauled from the river during dry spells. In wet weather it was obtained by placing a bucket or upturned helmet beneath the edge of the tent flap to catch the runoff. Many soldiers shaved sitting on their cots, their helmets filled with water, in front of small steel mirrors nailed to a corner post.

For bathing, soldiers had their choice of the swift-flowing brown river, or showers pumped up from the river through a pipeline. The major problem at either bathing point was the same—getting socks and shoes back on without getting dirty feet again.

There were two schools of thought on the laundry problem. One held that washing clothes was easy, and that there was no sense paying for laundry. The lazier group believed in using that time for an extra forty winks while natives did the work for money.

About half those who did their own laundry let it pile up and then boiled the lot in a halved gasoline drum. The other half—usually city boys—found it simpler to wash their clothes while swimming. Some dove in fully clothed except for shoes, using their bodies as washing boards.

One of our cooks set up a jungle laundry service for the lazy, running it on his off-duty time. With clotheslines of field wire, and halved gasoline drums for boilers, he made an extra $20 a day to add to his $28-a-month private's pay. When I asked him what he intended to do with all the money—a lot, in those days—he replied with a sigh, "Man, after the war—six terrific months in Havana!"

*   *   *

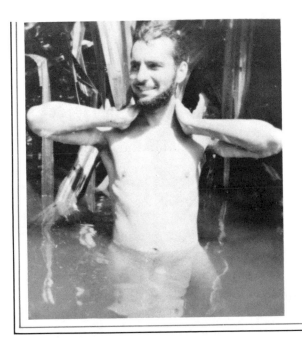

The author keeps clean in New Guinea.

Papuan natives doing laundry.

"How's it goin', Sad Sack?"

"Sweatin' it out, boy, sweatin' it out."

That standard reply was the most picturesque description possible for life on the violent-tempered island for thousands of bare-torsoed soldiers. Whatever the matter of the moment, they were usually "sweating it out," figuratively and literally.

Outside of twenty enemy bombers overhead, or one reveille formation, nothing would induce the New Guinea GI to rise at a bitter dawn hour for breakfast except fresh eggs. You could always tell when some had arrived by the size of the chow line. Each man would sweat out the hope that the supply would last until he reached the KP doling out the eggs.

Getting paid required sweating out another long line to sign the payroll and, a few weeks later, sweating out the payroll queue. If your name was Zimmerman, you really sweated out both lines.

Sweating out mail call required, first, waiting for the infrequent arrival of mail. When it did come, each name called out that did not happen to be yours hit like a slap in the face—that bundle held one less letter for you. If none of the letters bore your name, you returned to your tent disconsolately to begin sweating out the next mail call.

One of the most agonizing things to sweat out was promotion. Because privates, corporals, and sergeants were subject to pulling KP, sergeants sweated out promotion to staff sergeant to escape this unpleasant servitude.

If the incredible happened and a GI's name went up on a furlough roster, he began sweating out the schedule of names ahead of his. If he had to wait until some returned from Australia, he sweated out their being able to get transportation. When the day finally came that he rushed to Milne Bay or Moresby, full of bon boyage and

Aussie currency, he was asked for his air priority. Having none, he might have to sweat out a flight to Australia for a month and a half. If he finally had to leave by ship, he sweated out typhoons and enemy subs. If he flew out on a battered old DC-3, he sweated out the cough in the number-one engine.

Entertainment-hungry GIs also sweated out the movies that were shown in the jungle. Inexperienced soldiers handling the projectors often bollixed up the operation. The film would get the jiggers, with the stars jumping up and down on the screen, then blurring and fading out. Or the sound would fade to a whisper, or blare like thunder.

As jungle humidity rotted our clothing, many of us sweated out new issues. We were often reduced to living with one pair of pants, two pairs of socks, one undershirt, and two pairs of trunks. One GI who came to medical attention because of a limp was found to have a heel missing from his only pair of shoes.

The major spare-time hobby of most GIs was making souvenirs. Some soldiers were proficient enough to turn out great numbers to meet the demand. One popular gadget was a letter opener in the shape of a sickle. The handle was a Japanese .25-caliber rifle shell, split at the head. The blade, soldered into the head, was a 75-mm artillery shell, flattened, curved, and sharpened with a hammer and cold chisel. Artistic metalsmiths engraved their blades with the name "New Guinea." Each letter opener took about half a day to make and sold for $3.00 to $5.00.

Coin bracelets for Yanks enjoyed a lengthy vogue in the jungle. At first Australian currency was used with a large florin as the centerpiece, flanked by shillings and threepence pieces. (The currency has since changed.) Links for the bracelets were made by cutting threepences with tin shears and bending them into shape. When the first Japanese currrency was captured, enemy coin bracelets became popular.

The amateur jewelers were no less skillful in making rings. For days on end, when the war was relatively quiet, the camp would resound with the monotonous clank of hammers on coin edges. When the coin's rim was flattened sufficiently, the inside would be cut away and the ring filed and sandpapered. Rings were also made of thick plastic salvaged from windows of wrecked planes, and of aluminum from shot-down Zeros. Watch straps made of Zero aluminum commanded a good price as symbolic mementos.

Like other units, our platoon had its own barber shop. Our hair stylist was an Alabama farmer with two clippers and a scissors. He mounted a board swivel seat which pivoted on a tent spike protruding from a stump. Customers paid 30¢ for a ride and haircut. A favorite style was the Indian war-bonnet haircut, with all the hair shaved off except a high strip down the middle.

Pets gave the camp a homelike atmosphere. When our outfit had been stationed in Australia, we had adopted a cockatoo, a wallaby, and a Sydney Silkie poodle as mascots. During our hitch in Milne Bay, our favorite pets were flying squirrels. The GIs would chase them from one coconut tree to another, banging at the base of the tree with sledgehammers to frighten the squirrels into flying off. Eventually the squirrels tired out and were captured.

GIs who caught flying squirrels kept them in their shirt pockets, flaps buttoned. Our company clerk placed his pet on a stationery file on his desk. A book absent-mindedly jammed into the file ended their relationship. My own pet was a large green praying mantis that used to ride on my shoulder. It was so tame that it ate crumbs from my fingers. One day while I was washing my mess

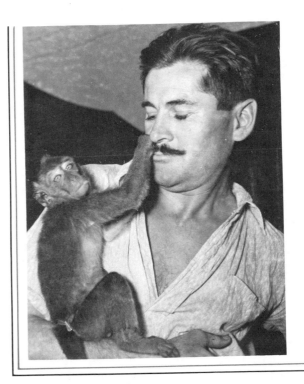

A Yank and company mascot, Tojo, who chews gum and pulls hair.

kit in a tub of boiling water, the mantis, sadly, lost its hold and fell in.

The most unusual pet of all was a small native boy adopted by an Air Corps major as group mascot. The boy wore a gold eagle emblem as a pendant and rode in jeeps and even planes. He enjoyed himself so hugely that when his mother came to claim him, the little mascot held her off with a knife and insisted that she let him remain where he was.

Tent dwellers liked to identify themselves as private clubs with humorous names like "Goldbrick Society" (society of job goof-offs), or "Volunteers for Alaska." One tent's occupants called themselves the "Section 8 Club." In Army slang, "bucking for a Section 8" meant acting "troppo" or "jungle-happy" to get an instant discharge on grounds of insanity.

The music-lovers in our outfit weren't frustrated by the lack of musical instruments. One GI made a fine-sounding banjo out of a powdered-milk can, telephone wires, and boxwood, and used the handle of a toothbrush as a bridge. He burned holes in the boxwood, then inserted plugs and attached his wires. Pieces of shot-down Zeros supplied his frets. The music was fine.

Writing letters home was a major preoccupation during off-duty hours. To many soldiers the task was an ordeal, since they could think of little to say that the Army censor would not delete. They were not even permitted to tell where they were.

When one of our GIs exhibited a gift for filling out two or three pages with bland, censorproof prose, his letter was passed around and copied by less imaginative comrades. Men with a facile pen were sought after by soldiers with important letters to write—sympathy notes, letters to fickle or indecisive sweethearts, and so forth. Our average GI was a whiz at doing or talking, but suffered intense torture when compelled to take up his pen.

Almost all of us sent home native gifts—grass skirts, hair combs, shell necklaces, and woven palm baskets.

Sports provided another welcome diversion in the jungle. Basketball courts were built from logs and packing wood. Plywood and lumber provided the material for ping-pong tables. Sports kits supplied by Special Services included some equipment for volleyball and baseball.

One group of GIs dug up a loudspeaker, ran a wire to the radio in the orderly tent, and enjoyed news and music on their cots. To foster community spirit and for the entertainment of all units in the area, the base used a

GIs at Milne Bay clown around in gift native skirts.

special frequency to put on a local radio program that featured camp talent.

The secret of American soldiers' remarkable adaptability to the bizarre and difficult environment of the jungle was their desire to recreate for themselves the comforts and pleasures they had left behind at home. Since they couldn't *be* at home, they did the next best thing and *made* themselves at home—at least as much as the jungle would allow.

One Christmas Eve our platoon put on a talent show in the grass-roofed mess hall. Two GIs put on an exhibition of jitterbug dancing to a harmonica accompaniment. Received with enthusiastic applause and delighted laughter, one of the panting dancers acknowledged the ovation.

"If only our mothers could see us now," he told the GI audience. "Two Brooklyn hepcats jiving in a Pacific jungle on Christmas Eve!"

14

Joining the Jolly Rogers

Although my adjustment to life in the Markham Valley was a smooth one, I anticipated difficulties if I remained with the platoon after I had forced the departure of Lieutenant Baxter. Battalion headquarters was none too pleased with my example as an enlisted man who challenged and deposed an incompetent officer. "You didn't handle it right," the company C.O. reproached me tartly.

It was decided that I should be transferred to headquarters, which had now moved up to Lae. Obviously, the brass wanted to keep an eye on a controversial master sergeant who had sought to protect his men from abusive, arbitrary orders.

Since my usefulness to the platoon was over, I decided to transfer out to the Air Corps. From flying with Air Corps units whenever I could as a war correspondent, I had come to have enormous respect for flying officers. I greatly admired the inspiring esprit de corps I found in Air Corps outfits.

There was a democratic relationship between officers and enlisted men, who often addressed each other by first name. The officers asked nothing of flight and ground crews except that they do their jobs well and courageously. The lives of all depended on that one requirement. No one bothered with the petty regulations that had made life intolerable for my men.

As a war correspondent I had gone on a number of missions in 90th Bomb Group Liberators. On my first B-24 mission, after drawing a flying suit and boots, I found my hands freezing and eyes tearing at 20,000 feet. The oxygen mask—there were no pressurized cabins in those days—made breathing difficult and unpleasant. The cold burned my cheeks and the intercom headset hurt my ears for the two-and-a-half-hour flight. I returned with new respect for the men who, in extreme discomfort, risked their lives on each mission.

I also did a story on the B-25 Mitchell Marauders, medium bombers that were often used for skip bombing—flying low over enemy shipping and land targets for greater accuracy. I flew with one pilot who was making some kind of test run. I settled myself in the tail of the plane over a glass observation panel.

We barely skimmed treetops along the coast and stayed at that level all through the flight. I watched parachutes with bombs attached fall away beneath my nose, disappearing into the jungle below. After a moment or two there were terrific explosions. When we returned to base the pilot asked me from what vantage I had watched the bombings. I told him I was in the tail.

"Great Scott!" he exclaimed. "Didn't you know that this was a test run for delayed-action bombs? We weren't sure whether they'd work properly. If they'd gone off on contact, you could have been killed!"

From then on I made sure I had a clear understanding beforehand of the nature of any flights I joined.

On January 6, 1944, I started to type an application for transfer to the Air Corps. My C.O. refused to let me use the typewriter. I pointed out that my letter was official business. Ripping the page out of the typewriter, he tore it to pieces. I took a deep breath and reminded him that there were other typewriters I was entitled to use as a war correspodent.

I left headquarters and walked down the road toward the sign that marked the site of the 90th Bomb Group. The group's four-engined Liberators were marked with a grinning skull and crossed bombs on their huge tails. Named after their first commander, they were known as the Jolly Rogers. The unit was one of the star groups of the Fifth Air Force, which was under the command of General George C. Kenney. Kenney's skill at using bombers to sink Japanese shipping caused MacArthur to refer to him admiringly as "a twentieth-century pirate."

I went to see Colonel Harry J. Bullis, then their C.O., and asked to transfer into the group.

"I'm afraid our T.O. [table of organization] doesn't allow us any more master sergeants," he told me.

"I'd be glad to transfer in as a private," I shrugged.

He looked astonished. "But why?"

I told him. "I'm sick and tired of fighting the Army instead of the enemy," I added. "I want to be part of an outfit where the enlisted men and officers cooperate to do a real job for the war effort. Can you use another hand to push oil barrels around on the airstrip?"

"We don't really need any more field crew. But you're a war correspondent, and we *do* need someone who can cover news stories about our missions for the fliers' hometown newspapers."

He urgently requested my services on temporary duty, pending my official application to the Fifth Air Force for a transfer. When I presented the Colonel's written request to the captain of my company, he read it with a curled lip.

"Air Corps!" the C.O. sneered. "Civilians in uniform!"

"Exactly," I smiled. "That's what I want to be—one of those overseas civilians in uniform who are really fighting the war, instead of a member of a close-order drill squad that excels in saluting."

He had no alternative but to honor Colonel Bullis's request. "At least," he said, "there's some satisfaction in knowing you'll pay for your insubordination by being reduced to a private."

Campsite of the Jolly Rogers in Nadzab.

I joined the Jolly Rogers on January 18, 1944, on temporary duty. Soon afterward, Fifth Air Force replied to my request for an official transfer as a private—they refused it. No master sergeant could request a reduction in rank for himself, Fifth Air Force ruled, because too much expensive training had gone into the making of a six-striper.

Shrugging, Colonel Bullis decided to transfer me in officially as a master sergeant. So I spent my final year-and-a-half overseas in the Air Corps, respecting and cooperating with officers instead of having to struggle against them.

In their first year of battle, the Jolly Rogers had destroyed more enemy aircraft than any other bomb group in the Pacific theater. Their gunners had shot down 320 enemy planes in the air, and their bombs had destroyed hundreds more on the ground and sunk 52 enemy ships.

Jolly Rogers crewmen, originally based in northern Australia, had seen battle quickly and had had more than their share of hair-raising experiences. After one

The author as a GI war correspondent.

combat mission in which a B-24 was badly shot up, it failed to return to base, crash-landing in the jungles of Australia's Northern Territory.

All but four of the crewmen were killed. The four climbed out of the wreckage, dazed and trembling. In their search for a way out of the jungle, three of them weakened and died. The fourth, S/Sgt. Grady Gaston of Frisco City, Alabama, wandered through the jungle for 141 days, living on snakes, fish, and crocodiles.

When he was finally found after almost five months, he had lost sixty-eight pounds and was delirious. Amazingly, he lived.

Gaston's survival was an inspiration to Jolly Rogers crews. "See?" they encouraged each other. "Even if you get shot down, you've always got a fighting chance."

Typical of the spirit that animated the group was the crew of the *Mission Bell*, which went on an armed reconnaissance mission over Wewak to search for a missing B-24. It was attacked by eighteen Zeros. The *Mission Bell*'s gunners fought them off with red-hot barrels, shooting four Zeros down in flames, with three more "probables." Four members of the crew were wounded. The big bomber collected four hundred bullet holes and had one engine shot out and two others on reduced power, a wingtip shot up, both ailerons useless, the tail turret out, radio out, holes in all the gas tanks, and five bullet holes through the left tire. And the right tire blew out on landing.

Yet the *Mission Bell* made it back safely.

On their last combat mission, the crew was part of a six-plane raid on Wewak, with P-38s flying top cover. Thirty Zeros attacked, driving two B-24s out of the formation. The flight leader dropped back to protect them. Zeros pounced on the isolated *Mission Bell*. A 20-mm burst through its waist, knocked out the hydraulic system, splashed hydraulic fluid all over the plane, and ignited one of the flares.

Waist gunner S/Sgt. Donald O. Crandall of Bloomfield, Iowa, realized that if the fluid reached the flare, the plane would be blown to pieces. With his bare hands he pulled the burning flare from the rack, kicked a hole in the camera door, and threw the flare out. As he did this, machine-gun fire raked the waist of the bomber, wounding Crandall in the leg and arm. He limped back to his gun and shot down his second Zero of the day.

It was that kind of outfit.

Top turret gunner T/Sgt. Frank A. Matthews, Jr., of Elma, New York, displayed similar heroism when his Liberator, the *Eager Beaver*, failed to release its bombs over the target.

Matthews descended from his turret and hung head-down into the roaring winds of the open bomb bay while radio operator T/Sgt. Kenneth B. Rickert held his legs. Matthews succeeded in prying two bombs loose with a screwdriver.

The *Eager Beaver* was suddenly attacked by Zeros. Rickert hastily pulled Matthews up, and the gunner returned to the top turret. After a fifteen-minute fight the Zeros were driven off. Matthews then returned to the open bomb bay to try to loosen the rest of the bombs. Swaying in the freezing gale at 24,000 feet, he began to lose consciousness. Rickert quickly shoved an oxygen mask down to him. Matthews succeeded in releasing the rest of the bombs.

One Jolly Rogers Liberator was flying reconnaissance off the north coast of New Guinea when the pilot sighted an enemy convoy. As he headed for it, the B-24 was suddenly attacked from all directions by fifteen Zeros whose guns blazed at close range. The pilot was killed by 20-mm cannon fire crashing through the windshield. Shrapnel hit everyone on the flight deck, wounding co-pilot 1st Lt. Robert B. Yonker of Bellingham, Minnesota, in the face and hands.

A powerful gale rushed through the smashed windshield, turning the flight deck into a blurred chaos of roaring wind, smashed equipment, and blood-smeared windows. Rousing himself from the shock of his wounds, Yonker peeled the B-24 off toward some thin cloud cover as the Zeros pressed home more attacks. All the bomber's communications were shot out.

Unable to see out the blood-spattered windows, with shrapnel burning his face, Yonker flew the plane against the furious gale with his head out the side blister. A Zero tried to block the B-24's escape but was shot down by the nose gunner. Yonker managed to hide the bomber in some clouds.

As the bombardier helped stanch Yonker's wounds and the radio operator cleaned the windows, Yonker continued to fly the plane in a state of severe shock. He landed it safely, despite having had a left rudder shot away. In addition to his Purple Heart, he was awarded an Air Medal with two Oak Leaf Clusters.

Ingenuity saved some crews from disaster. One crew gave credit to the camp PX for saving their lives. They had been flying a long-range mission over Matsuyama, Formosa. Ack-ack fire proved exceptionally heavy, and an enemy shell punctured the valve of the B-24's auxiliary gas tank. Gasoline they would need for their return was spurting down to the China River below.

The crew's only chance, it seemed, was to bail out.

Pilot 1st Lt. Harry Hurst of Houston, Texas, thought fast. His copilot, notoriously nervous over the target, always chewed gum that he bought by the carton from the PX. A fresh stick popped into his mouth each time a burst of ack-ack came too close. Now Hurst commandeered his copilot's carton of gum, turned the controls of the B-24 over to him, and went back to join the engineer, T/Sgt. Newell S. Williams of Old Fort, Tennessee.

Williams, with all his tools and materials, had not

been able to stop the fatal leak in the valve. At the rate they were losing gas, Hurst knew they could never make it back to the nearest American emergency landing base. He explained his idea to Williams. Then the two men began chewing gum at a furious pace, collecting each wad into a sticky bundle.

Finally they had enough to gum up the leak. During the half-hour struggle they were drenched with gasoline and had to wear sunglasses to keep the gas out of their eyes. But thanks to the PX chewing gum, the B-24 retained enough gas to get safely back to an emergency landing base.

When the Jolly Rogers joined in a huge raid on Rabaul, one B-24 was shot up so badly that the crew had to take to parachutes when the plane failed to make it back to base and crashed in the jungle. Friendly natives reunited the crewmen at a nearby village. To let rescue planes know where they were, the crew used towels, sheets, shirts, and parachutes to make a large replica of the Jolly Rogers' insignia on the ground.

The skull and crossed bombs were easy to represent in cloth, but the eyes and mouth of the skull presented a problem. The crew solved it by having one native sit in the place of each eye and another stretch out to represent the mouth. The insignia caught the attention of a reconnaissance plane. Two weeks later the crew was rescued.

Narrow escapes were the order of the day with the Jolly Rogers. On a reconnaissance mission over Kavieng one afternoon, Capt. Everett A. Wood, Jr., of Trinidad, Colorado, piloted his B-24 through antiaircraft fire "so thick you could walk on it," as he related later. All four engines were hit and started to malfunction.

"Doesn't look as though we'll make it back, boys," he told the crew over the interphone. "Do you want to land down there and give ourselves up as prisoners?"

Photo taken by a Jolly Rogers aerial photographer of the bombing raid on Rabaul.

"Who's got a deck of cards?" asked the copilot dryly. "Looks like we're in for a long session of rummy."

"Hey, Ev, I think we could make it back," said the engineer. "Why don't we give it a shot?" The crew voiced their approval.

Wood turned for home. With his fuel indicator shot out, he had no way of telling how much gas was left. Throughout the long trip back, the engineer kept siphoning gas from one fuel tank to another. Able to use only two engines at a time, they used them sparingly.

There were cheers when they finally saw a gleaming ribbon of silver beneath them—their base runway. Wood nosed the big bird in for a crash landing. The plane was smashed beyond repair, but its crew of eleven walked away unhurt.

15
Heroism in the Sky

Many of the crews were heroic, performing acts far beyond the call of duty. One B-24, loaded with bombs, crashed on takeoff. One motor burst into flame and a second roared dangerously with a bent propeller. The stunned aerial photographer, S/Sgt. J. Philip Bambara of Chicago, found he was the only one left in the plane but was too bewildered to save himself.

The pilot was Lt. Col. Harry J. Bullis of Portland, Michigan, who later became C.O. of the Jolly Rogers. He dashed inside and roused Bambara, then risked his life further by extinguishing flames in the engine.

On another occasion Bullis was leading a flight of three B-24s in search of enemy shipping near Ambon Island. Spotting their target, the Liberators peeled off for individual attacks. Suddenly nineteen Zeros dove out of the clouds, firing on Bullis's bomber and killing the left waist gunner.

A lone B-24 had no chance against nineteen swirling Zeros. As Bullis swerved to escape, the enemy planes buzzed around the Liberator like angry hornets. His only chance lay in combining fire power with one of the other Liberators, so he called for the pilot ahead to slow down. The pilot decelerated so quickly that Bullis's plane shot past him. Half of his tormentors left him to pounce on the other Liberator.

The two planes finally managed to get together and fight off the enemy as a team. Then they headed back to join forces with the third B-24, but it zoomed past both of them in the opposite direction. The flealike Zeros promptly deserted the teamed B-24s for the easier lone prey.

A formation of Jolly Rogers B-24s Liberators take off for a strike against the enemy.

Major Charles Whitlock, one of the best Jolly Rogers pilots, who later became Dean of Harvard.

At last all three Liberators managed to get together and sent four Zeros plunging to the ground. Bullis's bomber had an engine shot out, but he took it back safely and made a perfect landing on a flat tire he didn't know he had.

Sometimes the forbidding mountains of New Guinea were even more dangerous than the enemy. When the weather turned foul during one reconnaissance mission, 1st Lt. Henry Girner headed out to sea following the coastline until clouds obscured his vision. When he reached the point he considered parallel to his destination, he turned inland.

He gradually reduced altitude for a run over the target, an enemy air base. Abruptly the clouds parted before him. Girner's jaw dropped. He was heading almost directly into a mountain.

He swiftly cut his automatic pilot and stood the twenty-ton bomber on its tail. The weather observer's head slammed against the ceiling and he nearly lost consciousness. The rest of the crew spilled around the plane like a dropped boxful of toothpicks.

The B-24's wings actually scraped branches off treetops, and leaves flew into the engines. But they made it. Trembling and perspiring, Girner didn't stop climbing until the altimeter read a safe 18,000 feet.

Another close call on reconnaissance was registered by Capt. Tom C. Hanzel of Faribault, Minnesota, who was ordered to take photos of Japanese warships in the Bismarck Sea. Enemy naval guns shot away all the B-24's hydraulic lines, starting a bad gas leak. Hanzel didn't dare jettison his bombs for fear that sparks would set off an explosion. Gas fumes filled the bomber. As rapidly as they could, the crew transferred fuel out of the leaking tank, then cleared the fumes from the plane.

Hanzel salvoed the bombs and turned for home. He was forced to crash-land without brakes or flaps. As a final touch, the nosewheel snapped on landing, sending the crew sprawling. But, aside from one gunner wounded by enemy ack-ack, the crew survived without serious injury.

When 1st Lt. Stuart F. Hutson of St. Augustine, Florida, flew an armed reconnaissance mission over enemy shipping north of New Britain, miserable weather forced his plane down to a dangerous five hundred feet. Spotting the enemy convoy they were seeking, Hutson piloted the B-24 toward it through a fierce barrage of 40-mm. antiaircraft fire. One shell exploded squarely in the B-24's bomb bay. The crew held their breath.

The bombs didn't explode. Then hot shrapnel splintered the gas tanks. The crew prayed. The gas didn't explode.

With his hydraulic power and instruments shot out,

Hutson fought the controls as the plane lost power and altitude. He strove to hold it thirty feet above the ocean. Spray splashed the windshields as Hutson and his co-pilot struggled to keep first one, then the other wingtip from dipping under the waves. And all the while a fire raged in the bomb bay.

The crew couldn't extinguish the fire. Neither could they jettison the bombs, because the bomb bay doors wouldn't open.

Just when it seemed certain that the crew would perish in either an ocean crash or a terrible bomb blast, land appeared—an Allied base with a clearing. Hutson swerved the B-24 and touched down swiftly for an emergency landing.

Tumbling out safely, the crew was too busy with grateful prayers to heed the bawling out they received for having caused a Red Alert at the base by flying in unidentified.

Crewmen who manned the bombers' guns never knew whether they would be alive the next morning.

T/Sgt. Joseph A. Lepa of Manchester, New Hampshire, joined the Air Corps as a tail gunner nine days after his brother Stanley had been shot down and killed in a Liberator over France.

On one mission lightning struck his plane, enveloping it in a blinding blue flame. The radio equipment was instantly burnt to a crisp. Although the crew jumped a foot in the air, no one was hurt. When the plane reached its target and dropped its load, Zeros attacked. In the excitement Lepa accidentally kicked the crew's box of sandwiches and tinned fruit through the open bomb bay. Over the interphone the crew wryly discussed the possibility of sending Lepa after them.

Lepa's tightest spot was over Rabaul. His bomber was persistently attacked by enemy planes for an exhausting forty-five minutes. All his guns went out of commission. Lepa and the others put on an act, manipulating their .50-caliber machine guns ferociously to give the impression of holding fire until the Zeros came in close enough. Their bluff, aided by firepower from other planes in the formation, saved them from being shot down.

Sgt. Ray Fitzgerald of New Albany, Mississippi, was the engineer on a B-24 mission over Madang when an enemy shell smashed through the fuselage three feet in front of him. Fortunately missing the oxygen tanks, the shell flew out the other side and burst a hundred feet above the plane. A second shell sliced the aileron control cables. The bomber sideslipped out of control.

Thinking fast, Fitzgerald climbed out on the catwalk of the open bomb bay. As the bomber lurched like a drunken sailor, he swiftly stripped arming wires out of some bombs and used them to splice the severed aileron cables. His patch job restored a ragged but effective con-

Author and a Jolly Rogers crew inspect the tail of a shot-up Liberator.

trol to the pilot, who was then able to fly the plane safely back to base.

The world was stunned when it heard of Japanese kamikaze pilots who turned themselves into suicidal flying bombs, diving their planes into American warships. First Lt. Leland E. Minor, a navigator from El Monte, California, encountered a kamikaze in the air. His Liberator was under attack in a mission over Rabaul when he noticed one Zero flying toward him in what seemed to be a close pass. But at the last moment he realized that the enemy flier had no intention of swerving. In a few seconds the Zero would crash into him in a deadly embrace.

Minor shouted a warning. The pilot, suddenly alerted, made a desperate effort to bank sharply to the right. The Zero hurtled past, skimming them by a bare five feet. The kamikaze pilot was shot down by the waist gunner of a nearby B-24.

Flying a mission near the enemy-held Admiralty Islands, 1st Lt. Robert J. MacVittie of Utica, Michigan, lost an engine and found his rudders locked. While he struggled to hold the bomber straight, it dropped steadily until they were only 450 feet above the sea. He ordered their bombs salvoed.

The blast from the explosion released the locked rudders. But, although they were then able to fly straight, the plane continued to lose altitude.

"Throw out everything you can!" MacVittie shouted over the intercom. The crew quickly jettisoned guns, ammunition, bomb hoists, and camera. The bomber nevertheless continued dropping to 400 feet . . . 350 feet . . . 300 feet . . . 250 feet. . . .

"Prepare to abandon ship!" MacVittie called.

Two hundred feet above the waves, the Liberator suddenly leveled off. MacVittie, holding his breath and praying, coaxed every ounce of power from the ailing

The Jolly Rogers B-24 named after Harry S. Truman when he became president.

bomber. He managed to stay 200 feet above a watery grave while he nursed it back to base.

Japanese fliers had their own narrow escapes flying missions out of New Guinea. Naval Aviation Pilot First Class Saburo Sakai told about his, long after the war was over. He had taken part in the attack on Clark Field in the Philippines and shot down the first American pilot lost there. He had once flown on a kamikaze mission, but he had been spared suicide when a storm had forced his echelon to return to base.

Stationed with a squadron of Zeros at Lae, Sakai had shot down sixty-two American planes before his luck ran out. Attacking American bombers near Guadalcanal, the enemy ace brought down two fighter planes, exposing himself dangerously to do it. Two .50-caliber machine-gun rounds shattered his canopy, sending shrapnel ricocheting off his goggles and into his forehead.

"What happened after that proves the power of desperate human beings," he recalled. He had felt paralyzed and had lost consciousness. On its own, his Zero had miraculously avoided the ocean beneath. When Sakai came to, his plane was flying upside down about three hundred feet above the waves.

Blood filled his one good eye. He couldn't move one arm. With the other he stanched the wound with his silk scarf. His head wounds made it difficult for him to remain conscious, but he fought off the darkness that sought to engulf him as he flew his fighter more than 550 miles back to Lae.

"Human beings tend to be optimistic," Sakai said, "and we always think in terms of tomorrow. I always thought my turn to die was coming, but never today, always tomorrow."

Forty years later, he was still alive in Tokyo.

Ironically, many young American pilots died unnecessarily. Some in our group chafed at flying Liberators. "It's like driving a truck through the sky," one young man told me. "When I joined the Air Corps, I wanted to be a fighter pilot." On his free day he went over to an adjacent fighter squadron and got permission to take up a P-38 on a practice flight.

I watched him put the plane through a series of daring acrobatics. His last stunt was buzzing the camp at treetop level. In the next second he had crashed into power lines, and the sky lit up with the flames. He was only twenty years old.

Other restless young pilots died the same way.

Sometimes a gung-ho pilot would take his whole crew with him. Scheduled to return to the States after having completed their missions, the crew would agree to the pilot's suggestion of one last mission for good measure. In several cases the plane was shot down, and all aboard were lost.

In the darkest moments of combat, an airman's sense of humor sometimes came to his rescue.

On a daylight strike over Rabaul, 1st Lt. Robert H. Hallett of San Francisco found his B-24 under attack by a swarm of Zeros. An engine was shot out. The nose gunner's twin .50s jammed. More bad news came over the interphone from the tail gunner.

"Right gun jammed, left gun jammed. We're out of ammo. What do you want us to do now?"

Zeros were coming in at them all around the clock.

"Start using spitballs," Hallett suggested dryly.

On a night reconnaissance mission, moonlight flooded the skies as a Jolly Rogers B-24 headed for the enemy base at Hollandia. Waist gunner S/Sgt. Donald Trappler, a new recruit from Wauwatosa, Wisconsin, was keeping a sharp lookout for enemy night fighters. After a long, silent vigil, his muscles suddenly tensed. His fingers tightened their grip on the trigger of his gun.

"Right waist gunner to pilot. Enemy fighter at two o'clock, high. Get your guns on him, boys!"

There was an excited bustle among the gunners as they swung their muzzles toward two o'clock, high, then an ominous quiet.

Finally top turret gunner S/Sgt. Vincent W. Mason, of Darien, Connecticut, asked, "Where is he?" Calling from the nose, T/Sgt. Harold L. Tate, of Southern Pines, S.C., reported dubiously, "I don't see nothin'."

"You guys blind?" Trappler screamed angrily. "Look! Look! At two o'clock! Here he comes—watch him!"

He was about to fire when a laconic voice droned over the interphone: "Navigator to right waist gunner. Suggest you hold fire. Wait until planet Venus comes into range."

Bomb day doors wouldn't open when the Liberator in which nineteen-year-old radio engineer T/Sgt. Stephen D. Baldwin of Watertown, Connecticut, was flying reached its target. He was sent onto the catwalk to open the doors manually. Wearing his 'chute, he cranked the doors open. Flak began to pop under his feet, which were turning cold for more reasons than the high altitude.

As he tried to wriggle back to the flight deck, a strap of his parachute pack caught on one of the bomb racks. He couldn't reach up or turn around to disentangle himself. With no oxygen, his breath began to come hard. He felt his strength ebbing. The only thing that kept him from blacking out was the ominous *whoof* of the ack-ack probing closer and closer to his heels.

After what seemed an eternity, Baldwin saw the navigator, F/O G.I. Alberts, twenty-three, of Kenosha, Wisconsin, peering down at him. Overjoyed at the prospect of deliverance, Baldwin waved frantically and shouted for help. Alberts, who couldn't hear him, grinned approval—and waved back.

Groaning, Baldwin finally managed to struggle out of his tangled harness. Pulling his way back to the flight deck, he buried his face in an oxygen bottle. Alberts slapped him on the back and exclaimed in admiration, "Hey, it sure took nerve sitting that one out on the catwalk without oxygen. But I sure wouldn't try that again, if I were you!"

One morning 1st Lt. Edward A. Kluck, twenty-one, of New Haven, Connecticut, was piloting his Liberator on the track of an enemy task force to keep it in sight for the rest of the Jolly Rogers, who were to rendezvous with him later. As he began cursing his luck when clouds hid the convoy, a call came over the command set.

"Friendly Tracker calling Big Tail Five. You are now due southwest of task force. Veer twenty degrees right. Over."

"Big Tail Five to Friendly Tracker," Kluck replied gratefully to his unseen mentor. "Rajah and thanks. What is your position? Over."

*Clouds of smoke rise from war plants in Japanese-occupied Balikpa-
pen, the longest bombing raid flown by the Fifth Air Force's Jolly
Rogers B-24s.*

"Friendly Tracker to Big Tail Five. Position twenty-
one-thirty north at one-twenty-three."

Kluck scanned the skies to locate his informant. But
as far as he could see, his B-24 was alone in the sky.
Suspicious of an enemy trick, he called, "Big Tail Five to
Friendly Tracker. What is your altitude? Over."

There was no answer. Kluck repeated the question. At
last he received his reply.

"Friendly Tracker to Big Tail Five. Altitude minus
twenty feet." Kluck blinked in bewilderment. Then the
voice on the radio explained the mystery. "This is a Navy
submarine!"

Although war was a grim business, with lives lost
every day, flight crews desperately enjoyed every scrap
of humor they could find in their dangerous work.

When you laughed a lot, you forgot to be scared.

16

What Men Think of in the Face of Death

During my flights as a war correspondent, I found myself wondering what crewmen were thinking on missions that they knew might represent their last hours on earth. I decided to set up an experiment that would reveal their thoughts as they flew into combat.

I won the cooperation of a Jolly Rogers crew assigned to a major bombing mission over Hollandia, at that time the strongest enemy air base in the Southwest Pacific. We were part of an echelon assigned to "soften" the base for an Army invasion. We would be followed over the target by medium bombers. Our escort fighters were Lockheed Lightning P-38s.

The eleven airmen in the experiment were veterans of 250 combat hours and of 38 missions flown together. Before we took off, I explained my plan for the eight hours we would be airborne. Using the intercom, I intended to break in on each man's thoughts from time to time, without warning. I would suddenly ask, for example, "Nose gunner, what are you thinking about?"

I asked each man to report his thoughts honestly at that moment. The entire crew promised to cooperate. I usually let a period of silence elapse between questions. This allowed each man to pursue his own reflections without being influenced by the replies of the others.

I also took down, verbatim, the conversation I heard over the intercom. Recorded in this chapter are the actual thoughts and conversation of eleven crewmen during the four hours that preceded their appointment with possible death and the four hours following their victory over it.

The crew of the unusual mission flown by the author when he recorded their thoughts. Author is at top right. The pilot is at top right.

To distinguish between thoughts and conversation, I have transcribed the crewman's thoughts in italics.

The pilot of the Liberator was 1st Lt. Charles Koster, twenty-two, a Rochester, New York, stock clerk. The copilot was 1st Lt. Walter M. Severance, nineteen, a Flint, Michigan, student. The bombardier was 1st Lt. A. Warren Ownes, twenty-three, an Atlanta photographer. The navigator was 2nd Lt. J. P. MacDonald, twenty-two, a Pittsburgh cost recorder. The radio operator was T/Sgt. J. J. Hrivnak, twenty, a Purseglove, West Viriginia, cook. The photographer-gunner was T/Sgt. John Salek, twenty-three, a Wheeling, West Virginia, steel worker. Top turret gunner was T/Sgt. W. P. Harrison, twenty-three, an Ehrhardt, South Carolina, auto mechanic. Nose gunner was S/Sgt. Ralph E. Bower, thirty, a Sunbury, Pennsylvania, ship welder. Left waist gunner was S/Sgt. Herbert Pigors, twenty-six, a Groton, South Dakota, aircraft worker. Right waist gunner was S/Sgt. Roger A. Schwartz, twenty-three, an Evansville, Wisconsin, farmer. Tail gunner was S/Sgt. A. Braunstein, nineteen, a Brooklyn, New York, shoe worker. They were a typical cross-section of America.

We take off at 0740 hours. Many of us sweat out take-off crowded on the catwalk in the bomb bay, between racks holding several thousand pounds of bombs. This makes the tail lighter, helping pilot Koster get the bomber off the strip. After several minutes airborne, we take our respective positions in the plane, putting on our interphone headsets.

TAIL GUNNER (singing): Brt-rt-rt! Rosie the Riveter!

PHOTOGRAPHER: Already we have trouble. What a voice.

TAIL GUNNER: Jealous!

R. WAIST GUNNER: *Wonder if I ought to put on my Mae West* [life preserver] *today. Not much water to go over. Just over the target.*

NOSE GUNNER: *Gotta write some letters when I get back. Don't write any, won't get any.*

TAIL GUNNER: *Only two ships behind us. Guess one didn't take off.*

TOP GUNNER: *Wish I had a plate of baked beans, the way Mom makes 'em.*

NAVIGATOR: *Good weather. Looks like a nice clean mission.*

COPILOT: *There's that waterfall, at five o'clock. Like to go see it sometime.*

PHOTOGRAPHER: *Beautiful country down there. Bet it would be pretty terrible to get through, though.*

BOMBARDIER: *Wonder if we get jumped today.*

L. WAIST GUNNER (calling pilot): There's a P-47 showing off at our left wingtip.

PILOT (calling tail gunner): Are there three ships behind us in the formation?

TAIL GUNNER: Only two. One on each side of us. Two more a little way back.

PILOT: See another five-ship formation?

TAIL GUNNER: I'll look around. . . . Yeh, Lieutenant, I see 'em.

PILOT: Rajah. [Okay.]

RADIO OPERATOR: *Good picture last night. Sure wish Betty Grable was here.*

R. WAIST GUNNER: *Ride back and forth so much, you get to know every landmark in New Guinea.*

TOP GUNNER: *If that screwball on the right gets any closer, I'm gonna put my guns right on him.*

PILOT: *Guess I'll hook up my chute when we get close to the target. Could be rough today.*

NOSE GUNNER: *Wish we'd turn around and head straight for Frisco.*

RADIO OPERATOR (calling engineer): Gas leak in the bomb bay. Try it out.

TOP GUNNER: Probably that hose again. . . . (A moment's silence) It's all right now.

L. WAIST GUNNER: *Be fun telling the boys back home what it was like over here.*

COPILOT: *Darn good formation today.*

R. WAIST GUNNER: *Boys are probably working in the fields now, putting the crops in.*

PILOT: *Wonder what the devil happened. All the ships staying in formation!*

NOSE GUNNER: *Be a happy day when I hit Frisco. Envy those guys with three hundred hours in. Be happy myself, then.*

R. WAIST GUNNER: *How I used to hate the old man for getting me up in the morning to milk the cows. I wouldn't now.*

PHOTOGRAPHER: *Wish we had a few more gravy runs like Gloucester. That's the trouble. They start you off easy, and then the missions get harder.*

TAIL GUNNER: *Wonder how that malted's gonna taste at the PX. Just enough for a swallow, probably.*

NAVIGATOR: *Round and round. Criminy, why don't we ever fly a straight course?*

PILOT: *The guy on the right's flying all over the place. Thinks he's a recco* [reconnaissance]. *One of these days a Zero will shoot his tail off.*

NAVIGATOR: *Three more hours to the target.*

R. WAIST GUNNER: *Those clouds, like snow drifting over fences.*

RADIO OPERATOR: *Not much to think about. The Marines had plenty to think about in Tarawa. Probably didn't think till it was all over, though. Like us when there's action. Rather be up here, though, than down there.*

TAIL GUNNER: *The danger's worth it. This life's better than spit-and-polish in the States.*

TOP GUNNER (calling pilot): Check number two engine. Oil coming out on top.

PILOT: Don't see it.

TOP GUNNER: Heck, if that ain't oil, I don't know oil.

L. WAIST GUNNER: If it was, you could see it on the tail. No oil on the tail yet.

PILOT: Rajah.

COPILOT: *Wonder what the Japs think about when we come over.*

TOP GUNNER: *Like to have a picture of this formation to show my wife when I get home.*

TAIL GUNNER: *It'd sure be nice walking up Times Square now with a girl on my arm.*

RADIO OPERATOR: *Gee, my behind gets tired sitting so much.*

BOMBARDIER: *I can always pick out my bomb bursts from the others. They look prettier, somehow.*

COPILOT: *Beautiful day. Everything going okeydoke.*

TAIL GUNNER: *I'm always riding backwards. Everbody else but me and the engineer rides forwards.*

PILOT: *Formation's outa shape again. Wish they'd get together.*

TOP GUNNER: *Like to get a Zeke today. Tell my wife all about it.*

BOMBARDIER: *Funny not having seen my own baby. Those snapshots are no good. Wonder what he really looks like.*

NOSE GUNNER: *Ships ahead are keeping a nice formation. Wonder why we're so lousy at it.*

PILOT (calling crew): Pilot to crew. . . . Test-fire your guns. Be careful of the other ships.

The plane reverberates with thuds. The gunners report all their guns functional. The tail gunner hits his head in the turret during testing.

TAIL GUNNER: *Darn it, I do it every time!*

NAVIGATOR: *There's Kharkar Island. We're right on course.*

R. WAIST GUNNER: *Getting cold. Better put my boots on.*

The plane bounces heavily as we get caught in the propwash of the leading formation.

PILOT: *Blast 'em! Wouldn't happen if they'd fly the right altitude!*
BOMBARDIER: *Wonder what guys think about when they go down.*
NAVIGATOR: *Only place in the world where you can navigate by the clouds.*
TOP GUNNER: *Love to get me a Zero today.*
L. WAIST GUNNER: *Defense workers back home can't know what men in combat think about.*
RADIO OPERATOR: *Wonder how I'd bail out.*
BOMBARDIER: *Where I sit, I never see a Zeke shot down.*
COPILOT: *Gee, I'm hungry already. I'll bet we only get corned willie [hash] when we get back.*
PILOT: *Wonder if Owens [bombardier] will hit the target today.*
COPILOT: *Rather take my chances going down with the ship than bailing out.*
TOP GUNNER: *Wonder what's for chow? I'm starved.*
R. WAIST GUNNER: *Used to read in the papers about the war over here. Now I'm in it. Son of a gun!*
L. WAIST GUNNER: *Be over Wewak soon. Better get ready.*
TAIL GUNNER: *Sure like to see our P-38s show up.*
BOMBARDIER: *Be nice going back. Shower. Hamburgers. And a Coke. Wish Koster would turn on the heat.*

We're now at 9,500 feet. My fingers are beginning to tremble and I find it difficult to continue making notes.

COPILOT: *Bombers all around us. Hate to be them poor Japanese bastards today. Be something when we can take over a thousand bombers like they do in Europe.*
R. WAIST GUNNER: *Bet Ma has something good for dinner tonight. Boy, I wish I was home for it!*

NAVIGATOR: *Wonder if those guys up front know where the devil they're flying those planes.*

RADIO OPERATOR: *That's Anderson on the right. Hope Koster's watching his ship. I sure don't like the way he flies, especially in rough Guinea weather.*

L. WAIST GUNNER (calling copilot): Watch number one engine on that ship at nine o'clock. He's throwing off puffs of smoke.

TOP GUNNER: *That bunch flies a rotten formation.*

TAIL GUNNER: That guy's feathered a prop now. He's veering to the right now. *Worries me to see something like that.*

BOMBARDIER (calling navigator): How far to the target?

NAVIGATOR: Fifty-five minutes—165 miles. We'll be there about 1107 if we don't go too much around and around.

BOMBARDIER: How fast will we be going over the target? What air speed?

NAVIGATOR: Look, all I know is we won't be there until 1107—and maybe not then.

R. WAIST GUNNER: *Funny, the way nature makes clouds like animals. That one's a cattle dog. That's a cow. There's a hog.*

TAIL GUNNER: *Whee! Here comes the P-38s. About time!*

BOMBARDIER: *Hope there're no darn clouds over the target. I'm sick of clouds ruining my runs.*

PHOTOGRAPHER (calling navigator): P-38s all over the place! Where are we at now?

NAVIGATOR: Little way below Wewak.

We can see Lockheed Lightnings playing around us high above. Some glint like whit gnats, some like black, depending on how they wheel and bank in the sun.

TAIL GUNNER: *Keeping my eyes open from here on.*

NOSE GUNNER: *My gun's pointed right at that cloud. I'm ready if the Zekes come through.*

PILOT: *The ship with the feathered prop must have gone home. Don't see it in the formation.*

NOSE GUNNER: *Hope we shoot up some ships at Hollandia. Like to go down and strafe. Be swell to sink a transport.*

BOMBARDIER: *B-25s are following in after us. Hope we do a good job and make it easier on 'em. I got some friends on the Mitchells.*

TAIL GUNNER: Ship behind us has landing lights on.

NAVIGATOR: Maybe he thinks the ack-ack need lights to aim at us better.

L. WAIST GUNNER: Naw. He's just planning a snow job. Wants to tell 'em back home that the ack-ack was so thick he had to turn on his lights to see his way through.

R. WAIST GUNNER: *Native villages down there. Uncivilized. Must be an awful life. Nothing to look forward to. And stuck there till they die.*

NAVIGATOR: Fifteen minutes more to Hollandia.

BOMBARDIER: *Wish they'd get somebody in the outfit who knows how to run that movie projector. Breaks down every time.*

COPILOT: Two P-38s at nine o'clock. Two at three o'clock. Two at six. Man—P-38s all over the joint!

PILOT: *Won't be long now. One flight's turning out to sea.*

TAIL GUNNER: *Here come the B-25s and A-20s. They're early. Guess they'll circle here till we clear out.*

RADIO OPERATOR: Any interception today? Boys, if we get it, we're just tail-end Charlies!

NAVIGATOR: If we get intercepted, it'll be in about half an hour. That, gentlemen, will be just about 9:45 P.M. last night back in Pittsburgh.

COPILOT: Can't tell you how relieved I am to know that.

NOSE GUNNER: That island down there looks like Pittsburgh. Hey, can you make out what's burning?

PHOTOGRAPHER: Can't tell. Smoke looks like a ship on fire.

Now we are at 10,800 feet, the cold is intense, and my fingers are numb. I don't make any more notes for a while. I leave the flight deck a few minutes before we reach the target and make my way gingerly through the bomb bay to the waist windows. The photographer hooks a parachute around me. The leg straps won't fit, so I let them dangle. There isn't time.

PHOTOGRAPHER: Don't be nervous, chum. You probably won't have to use it.

R. WAIST GUNNER: That's Tadje over there. We wrecked that last week.

L. WAIST GUNNER: Here we go. . . . Hey, Archer, you'll get a better view if you sit over the belly gun hatch.

It is 1131 hours. The photographer straps himself to the sides of the bomber like a window cleaner and leans over his hatch with his long camera. I crawl to the belly gun hatch, lean over, and peer down. The waist gunners are taut at their guns, scanning the skies for Zeros.

Suddenly I see the bombs of the flight ahead explode beneath me. The earth winks and blinks with a dozen demonlike eyes. Snapping, crackling sounds assail my ears like a string of firecrackers. The jungle settlement below is covered with red darting flashes, like a spilled box of matches, one instantly igniting the other. Toadstools of black smoke spring up from the stabs of flame.

I can see puffs of ack-ack fire probing for us to knock us out of the skies. One or two come too close for comfort, but most fall short of our altitude.

I am startled again when our own bombs fall away beneath my nose, forming a design like endpapers for a book. There is a faint, wiry, whorling sound as arming wires rattle loosely in the windswept bomb bay. I watch the bombs' vanes spin off, then lose sight of them in a cloud. Later the flight behind us informs us that we smashed a jetty and warehouse, all bombs on target. The ack-ack keeps bursting all over the sky.

I think of the briefing of our mission, when the briefing officer told us, "Keep an eye open for Superior Private Second Class Yasha Tamajamo. He really throws the ack-ack up at you—he's bucking for Superior Private First Class."

As we pull away from the target, we see rising up at about 15,000 feet three huge columns of smoke, two black, one white, and elaborately curled like a Madame Pompadour wig. Fires are blazing everywhere below. No Zeros show up to attack us.

I return to the flight deck.

PHOTOGRAPHER: Boy, that was funny. No interception at all.

R. WAIST GUNNER: I was all set for it. Well, anyhow, I've had some shots at a Zeke. You never did, Braunstein.

TAIL GUNNER: Horsefeathers.

TOP GUNNER: Anybody see the ack-ack guns?

PILOT: Clouds hid 'em. But there were puffs from the warehouse.

TAIL GUNNER: *Worst part's over. Rest is a cinch.*

PILOT: Pilot to bombardier. Come up here, will you?

The pilot and bombardier discuss probable results of the bombing.

TOP GUNNER: *Darn it. Didn't get a Zeke. Didn't even see one.*

COPILOT: *Not enough excitement over the target. Nothing going on. I'm hungry. Long time before we eat.*

RADIO OPERATOR (sending a report on the mission): *Hope this gets through the way I'm sending it.*
R. WAIST GUNNER: *We sure lit a lot of fires back there.*
NOSE GUNNER: Nose gunner to bombardier. Get me out of this freaking turret. My back's breaking.
TAIL GUNNER: Tail gunner to copilot. Can I open the turret door? I'd like to straighten up.
COPILOT: Copilot to tail gunner. Okay. Copilot to nose gunner. Bombardier's coming right down.
NAVIGATOR: Just think—they're eating chow in camp right now.
R. WAIST GUNNER: Why do we always get so hungry flying home?
RADIO OPERATOR: *Guard duty tonight. It ain't fair. Not after flying a long mission like this.*
BOMBARDIER: *Boy, I'm glad we hit the target. I'm praying the photographer got those pictures.*
NOSE GUNNER: Can't figure out why we didn't even see a Zero.
PHOTOGRAPHER: Our top fighter cover, boy, that's why. We've got the best air corps in the world.
R. WAIST GUNNER: *Wish my brother could have been along today. He'd have gotten a big kick out of it.*
L. WAIST GUNNER: How'd you like to go dancing tonight, Braunstein?
TAIL GUNNER: Sure! And you could dance with the abos [the GI slang for aborigines].
R. WAIST GUNNER: Remember that beautiful babe I met at that dance in Salt Lake City? She was like wow!
NOSE GUNNER: Did you say like wow or like cow?
TOP GUNNER: *I hope we take the rest of our missions in this ship. Great turret.*
NAVIGATOR (adding distances): 120 . . . 125 . . . 115 . . . 320 . . .
TAIL GUNNER: *Nice to be going back, instead of up there.*

R. WAIST GUNNER: *My folks'll sure by happy when I come home.*
PILOT: *Hope we make a smooth landing.*

About now a reaction to the mission sets in. Everyone aboard is happy to have made it to the target and back without serious enemy resistance. For awhile they take over the intercom with jubilant clowning around that is clearly an expulsion of the tension that had held all of us in its grip on the way to the target, when we had no way of knowing how severely we would be attacked.

NAVIGATOR: Flash! Message for Hirohito [Emperor of Japan]. Honorable Majesty—go and get stuffed!
TAIL GUNNER: Redyo Tukyo calling. Today three-hundred Zeros intercepted Jolly Rogers attack on Hollandia, shot down seventy-one heavy bombers. Japanese lost one wing bolt. Thank you!
NAVIGATOR: Flash from MacArthur's headquarters! One hundred Liberators take off for air strike. Two hundred return. A great day for Uncle Sam!
TOP TURRET GUNNER (singing): "Off we go, into the bright blue yonder. . . . "

Everybody joins in except the copilot, who makes noises like an airplane engine. Afterward the crew sings several songs: *Wabash Cannonball," "Me and My Gal," "Bicycle Built for Two,"* plus a few bawdy Air Corps songs. Finally it is quiet. Everyone is bored. There's an hour or so of silence.

R. WAIST GUNNER: *Engines rumble nice. Like a train.*
BOMBARDIER: *Boy, I sure hope those pictures come out.*
R. WAIST GUNNER: *Be nice to telephone Ma. But I don't have to hear her voice and she don't have to hear mine. We know we think of each other anyhow.*

TAIL GUNNER: *B-24s look nice in formation. Powerful.*
PILOT: *Beautiful day out there. Nice clouds. I'm hungry.*
NOSE GUNNER: *Wonder why the Japs sent no fighters up.*
TOP GUNNER: *I sure hope there's at least one letter from my wife. At least a V-mail.*
PHOTOGRAPHER: *Wow, I'm tired. Won't we ever get back?*
COPILOT: *Be nice having a crew of my own some day.*
PHOTOGRAPHER (imitating the pilot's voice): Pilot to tail gunner. Over.
TAIL GUNNER (momentarily fooled): Tail gunner to pilot.
PHOTOGRAPHER: Tail gunner, blow it out your nose!
TAIL GUNNER: I can't, you idiot. I'm the tail gunner. You want the nose gunner!

This exchange sparks a new way to pass the time, with each crewman pretending to be someone else.

RADIO OPERATOR: Pilot to crew. I want a volunteer to climb out on the wing and brush those flies off.
NOSE GUNNER: Radio operator to pilot. I volunteer, sir!
PILOT: Pilot to engineer. Get out and put some grease on the wheels. I want a smooth landing.
COPILOT: Check the landing gear. If it isn't up, put it up. If it isn't down, put it down.
TAIL GUNNER: Nose gunner to pilot. I'll check the nose wheel. If it isn't locked, I'll use the key.
NAVIGATOR: Leave the nose wheel up. I want a Purple Heart.

Now we come over our home base. We take our place in the traffic pattern and keep cruising, waiting our turn.

It's hard to be so far away
　　From you at Christmastide,
But our bombs help to speed the day
　　I take that homeward ride.

So fill an empty glass for me
　　And drink to flying weather,
To a quick and thorough Victory
　　We'll celebrate . . . together!

A Christmas card composed by the author for the Jolly Rogers to be sent to crewmen's folks at home.

TOP GUNNER: Engineer to pilot. Hydraulic fluid leaking out. Nose wheel won't lock. Better go down and check it.

He isn't kidding. We are forced to stay in the air until the nose wheel is finally persuaded to lock. Even then other aircraft get priority, and we are driven off six times by a red light when we try to land.

PILOT: *Darn P-38s—always in the way. I'm starved.*
L. WAIST GUNNER: *It's a lot easier sweating out landings than takeoffs. No bombs aboard to worry about.*
R. WAIST GUNNER: *Bet Ma gets a feeling I've returned safe.*
COPILOT: *I never feel how tired I really am till it's all over.*
RADIO OPERATOR: *I'll get through my three hundred combat hours all right. I'm lucky.*

We land at 1530 hours, after almost eight hours airborne. The pilot taxis into our revetment. The bomb bay doors slide open.

TAIL GUNNER: All tickets, please. Hey, Schwartz, you chow hound . . . wait for me!

17

Victory in New Guinea

In 1944, with the Japanese on the defensive, the ground war in New Guinea was largely turned over to the Australians, with U.S. bomber support. MacArthur used most of the American infantry in his drive back to the Philippines.

The Aussies attacked one Japanese stronghold after another in Papua New Guinea. By April the last enemy base south of Wewak had fallen, and the Aussies continued to press north to secure the rest of Papua. In October they were able to invade the nearby island of New Britain for an assault on Rabaul.

By this time MacArthur had returned to the Philippines. The Battle of Leyte Gulf, the last and greatest naval battle of the Pacific war, resulted in a decisive defeat for the Japanese. It destroyed most of Japan's sea power, giving the United States control of the sea of Japan. The following month B-29 Superfortresses began to attack Tokyo.

Then in August 1945 the United States dropped the world's first atomic bombs on the Japanese cities of Hiroshima and Nagasaki. The Japanese militarists surrendered, and World War II came to an end.

Yanks and Aussies who had served in New Guinea in the early days of the war in the Pacific were proud that the war had first been turned around by the crucial Battle of Milne Bay, the first Allied victory against the Japanese.

After the war, Prime Minister Ben Chifley of Australia paid tribute to our expendable task force and what our unexpected victory had meant to the Allies' final triumph in the Pacific. He went to Milne Bay to dedicate a monument to the Aussies and Yanks who had fought there. The monument was set amid the white crosses, planted in the dank New Guinea soil beneath shattered palm trees, for comrades who had died together in what had been a genuine battle for freedom.

Suggested Further Reading

Clune, Frank. *Somewhere In New Guinea*. Philosophical Library, 1952.

Curth, Hank. *Papua New Guinea*. Jacaranda Press, 1968.

Eichelberger, Robert L. *Dear Miss Em: General Eichelberger's War in the Pacific*. Greenwood Press, 1972.

Greenfield, Kent Roberts. *Command Decision*. Harcourt, Brace, 1959.

Haugland, Vern. *Letter From New Guinea*. Farrar, Straus, 1943.

Johnston, George Henry. *Toughest Fighting in the World*. Duell, 1943.

Kenney, George. *General Kenney Reports; a Personal History of the Pacific War*. Duell, 1949.

Mayo, Lida. *Bloody Buna*. Doubleday & Company, Inc., 1974.

Milner, Samuel. *Victory in Papua*. U.S. Department of the Army, 1957.

Okumiya, Masatake and Jiro Korikoshi. *Zero!* Dutton, 1956.

O'Neill, Tim. *And We, the People; Ten Years with the Primitive Tribes of New Guinea*. P. J. Kenedy, 1961.

Souter, Gavin. *New Guinea; the Last Unknown*. Taplinger, 1963.

Steinberg, Rafael. *Island Fighting*. Time-Life Books, 1978.

Warner, Denis Ashton. *The Sacred Warriors: Japan's Suicide Legions*. Van Nostrand Reinhold, 1982.

White, Osmar. *Green Armor*. Norton, 1945.

Williams, Maslyn. *The Stone Age Island: New Guinea Today*. Doubleday, 1964.

Index

218

220

Radio Tokyo, 22, 29, 70
Red Alerts, 26, 35, 42–43, 46,
    97, 134, 136, 150, 151,
    152, 155
Rickert, T/Sgt. Kenneth B.,
    182
Roosevelt, Franklin D., 8, 23

Sago palm, 92
Sakai, Pilot First Class
    Saburo, 193–94
Salamaua, 22, 25
Salek, T/Sgt. John, 200–13
Salvation Army, 167
Sanananda, port of, 120–22
Schwartz, S/Sgt. Roger A.,
    200–13
Scotch Grays, 165
Sepik tribe, 85–86
7th Australian Division, 28,
    35, 102
Severance, 1st Lt. Walter M.,
    200–13
Shaggy Ridge, 125–27
Signal Corps, 11
    basic training, 14–18
Simon, Sgt. William Charles,
    130–34, 135
Singapore, 21
16th Australian Battalion,
    125–27
Slim, Field Marshal, 76
Solomon Islands, 23, 72
Stalker, Capt. Leonard, 131
Standard Operating
    Procedure for
  Fighter Sector operations
    (SOP), 150, 151

Tamajamo, Pvt. Yasha, 208
Tate, T/Sgt. Harold L., 195
3rd Battalion, 119
32nd Australian Division,
    100–5, 106, 107, 108, 109,
    110, 111–12, 119, 120, 122
Townsville, Australia, 23, 24,
    25–26, 27, 30, 33, 137,
    138–40
Trappler, S/Sgt. Donald, 195
"Troppo" behavior, 40–41
Truman, Harry S., 193
22nd Australian Battalion, 54

U.S. War Department, 122

Wada, Sgt. Kyoshi, 123–24
Wewak, 125, 181–82, 214
Whitlock, Maj. Charles, 188
Williams, T/Sgt. Newell S.,
    183–84
Wood, Capt. Everett A., Jr.,
    184

Yamamoto, Col. Hiroshi,
    104–5
Yaws, 93
Yonker, 1st Lt. Robert B., 182

Zeros (Japanese aircraft), 41,
    46, 55–56, 86, 108, 118,
    130, 134, 146, 172, 181,
    183, 187, 188, 190, 191,
    193, 207

About the Author

Jules Archer was born in New York City and attended the College of the City of New York. He wrote publicity for Universal Pictures and served in the Pacific as both a Master Sergeant and a war correspondent in World War II. He fought in the New Guinea Battle of Milne Bay, which marked the turning point in the war against Japan.

After the war Mr. Archer turned to free-lance writing, achieving a reputation for well-researched, absorbing magazine articles and books. Traveling extensively all over the world to gather his information, he has dined in a longhouse with the High Talking Chiefs of Samoa; had tea with two Australian Prime Ministers; climbed a live volcano by camel in the Canary Islands; swum the Seine in Paris at midnight; been arrested in Communist Romania in pursuit of a story; met secretly with dissidents in the Soviet Union; and run around the cities of China at dawn.

He has written over sixty books, among them *Epidemic!*, which won an award from the New York Academy of Sciences; *Watergate: America In Crisis; The Philippines Fight For Freedom; You Can't Do That to Me!, The Plot to Seize the White House; Famous Young Rebels, Superspies*; and his latest, *Winners and Losers; How Elections Work in America.*

In 1977 Mr. Archer moved from New York, where he had been an inveterate skier, to Santa Cruz, California, where he rollerskates along the Pacific, plays chess, writes, and teaches writing seminars at the University of California Extension.